Educator's Activity Book
ABOUT BATS

Bat Conservation International

Bat Conservation International, Inc.

Post Office Box 162603 • Austin, Texas 78716 • 512/327-9721

Dear Educator:

Bats are essential to the balance of nature, playing key roles in maintaining the diversity and quality of life on earth. Nearly a thousand kinds comprise almost a quarter of all mammals. They keep vast numbers of our most serious insect pests in check, and, in tropical areas, their pollination and seed dispersal activities are of enormous ecological and economic value.

Nevertheless, bats also rank among the world's most endangered animals. Almost 40% of our North American species are endangered or are candidates for such status. Like most wildlife, they suffer from habitat loss. However, the single most important cause of bat decline is often deliberate destruction by people who needlessly fear them.

As an educator, you are in a unique position to help. Children are naturally curious about bats, and, with a proper introduction, quickly learn to appreciate them. The craft projects, games, and other activities provided in this handbook are designed to make education fun and can be integrated easily into other classroom studies.

Because bats are misunderstood and intensely feared, they are ideal for teaching basic principles about prejudice and fear of the unknown. As children come to understand how wrong they can be about bats, they may be encouraged to question basic assumptions often made about other unpopular animals and even people. Finally, they must learn to appreciate that wild animals are fascinating but potentially dangerous if handled.

We deeply appreciate your help in enlightening a new generation about the importance of bats and our environment. We also thank the many educators who have played an important role in making this publication possible. Ideas for future materials are always welcome.

Sincerely,

Merlin D. Tuttle

Merlin D. Tuttle
Founder and Executive Director

Educator's Activity Book
ABOUT BATS

Bat Conservation International
Austin, Texas
1991

Rev. 10/1994

8282

TABLE OF CONTENTS

Activity Number and Name   **Page**

Acknowledgments   2

Introduction   3

Activity 1   Test Your Bat Q   4

Activity 2   Bat Attitudes   9

Activity 3   Bat Crossword Puzzles   13

Activity 4   Seeing with Your Ears   16

Activity 5   Close Encounter with a Bat   18

Activity 6   Going, Going, Gone   21

Activity 7   Bat Masks   25

Activity 8   Greetings from a Bat   30

Activity 9   Bat Cave Bulletin Board   34

Activity 10   What's for Dinner?   38

Activity 11   How a Bat Compares to Me   42

Activity 12   Bat Fruit Salad   44

Activity 13   Where's My Baby?   45

Activity 14   Bat Math   46

Activity 15   A Year in the Life of Little Brown Bats   47

Activity 16   Refrigerator Bats   52

Activity 17   Bat Rap   53

Activity 18   Bats in the Comics   55

Glossary   57

Topics Featured in Each Activity   59

Reading List   60

Educational Materials List   62

ACKNOWLEDGMENTS

Bat Conservation International is grateful to many for the efforts that have gone into the *Educator's Activity Book About Bats*. Primary support for this publication came from the Geraldine R. Dodge Foundation with an additional contribution from the Potts and Sibley Foundation. Their much appreciated assistance will enable thousands of youngsters across the country to learn the facts about bats before misconceptions become established.

Several BCI members made contributions to the activities included. We thank them for their ideas and commitment to bat conservation. Alphabetically they are, Kathleen Adkins for Activity 1, Jannel Cannon for Activity 17, Nina Ford for Activity 15, and Dorothy Weber for Activity 9. Activity 16 was adapted with permission from Ranger Rick's *NatureScope*, "Amazing Mammals, Part I," published by the National Wildlife Federation, copyright 1986, 1988. We also thank *NatureScope* magazine for its outstanding activity models which provided a basis for development of this publication.

Several production people are recognized for their tireless efforts in assembling the content of the activity book.

Project Coordinator:	Patricia A. Morton
Editor:	Mari Murphy
Technical Review:	Merlin D. Tuttle
Teacher Review:	Nona Sansom
	Molly Tull Ketchum
Artists:	Kathy Rottier, cover art
	Aletha Reppel, illustrations
	Edd Patton, cartoons
Typesetting and Layout:	Susan K. Hughes, Wordwright Associates
Printing:	Futura Communications, Inc.

INTRODUCTION

Objectives, activity types, and targeted grade levels are explained for each activity, and a list of materials is included. Grade level guidelines are suggested, though educators should make their own judgments about which are most appropriate for their classes. The activities can be used individually or as part of a study unit on bats. Before planning to use an activity it will be useful to page through the entire book and familiarize yourself with the background information provided in *all* of the activities. For example, Activity 1 includes a substantial introduction to bats, Activity 2 addresses myths, Activities 7, 9 and 10 introduce bat diversity and anatomy, Activity 12 covers some of the economic benefits of bats, and bat endangerment is discussed in Activity 6. Information from several activities can be combined and educators can build presentations or programs appropriate to their specific needs. For the educator's convenience, a list on page 59 names all the activities along with the topics featured.

Every effort was taken to provide accurate information for this general-focus bat publication. With nearly a thousand bat species known to science, it is extremely difficult to generalize for all bats. Educators wishing more detailed and precise information about bat species or ecology may refer to the reading list at the end of this publication or consult a library.

1 TEST YOUR BAT Q

Objective: *To test basic knowledge about bats*

Grades: *3-5*

Type of Activity: *Questionnaire*

Materials:
- *Copies of page 8*
- *Pencils*

Background Information

What most people believe about bats isn't even true. Because bats fly at night and are shy, they are difficult to understand. People fear most what they understand least. Lack of understanding and deliberate destruction are the most common causes of bat decline worldwide. The following text provides an introduction to bats.

Copy the one-page questionnaire (pre-test) and give to students prior to a study unit on bats or before a program. For example, use the questionnaire in combination with one of Bat Conservation International's audiovisual programs (see inside back cover). The text included here will assist in presenting key points on the importance of bats. Following a study unit or program, the questionnaires can be returned to students who should then be able to correct any errors (post-test).

Answer Key

A. True, 2, 6, 7, 10.

B. Circle all

C. Nearly 6 feet, a flying fox bat from Java

D. Bumblebee, the bumblebee bat from Thailand

E. 1,000

F. 40

G. Mammals

H. 1

I. Circle all

J. Everywhere except polar regions

K. Circle all

Bats: Our Allies

Bats are animals of extraordinary importance. Many are so essential that, without them, thousands of other plant and animal species could die out, threatening entire ecosystems from rain forests to deserts.

Yet despite their importance, bats are among the world's least appreciated and most endangered animals. For centuries, people have feared and persecuted bats, exterminating whole species and threatening the survival of many more.

Bats have been neglected even by scientists and conservationists. Although nearly 1,000 kinds comprise almost a quarter of all mammal species, bats are by far the least studied. They are found everywhere except for very dry deserts and polar regions, but bats are often ignored in conservation planning, seriously jeopardizing efforts to save rain forests and other important habitats.

Like most animals, bats suffer from habitat loss and environmental pollution, but the primary cause of their decline is wanton destruction by humans acting out of fear and ignorance. Bats filled the night skies long before we walked the earth, but their survival today requires that we learn to value them as essential allies, deserving of our respect and appreciation.

Many people still believe that bats are blind flying mice that carry diseases and become entangled in women's hair. But bats are more closely related to people than to mice, none are blind, and they are far too clever to entangle themselves in anyone's hair. Bats seldom transmit disease to people or pets, and our concerns should be no different from those we apply to other wild animals. Simply do not attempt to handle them, and there is little to fear.

Bats are among the most gentle, beneficial, and even necessary animals on earth. They occupy almost every habitat worldwide, eating insects, pollinating flowers, and dispersing the seeds that make rain forests grow. Forty-three species live in the United States and Canada, but the majority live in the tropics. Wherever bats are found, they are essential elements in nature's delicate web of life.

Controlling Insects: Masters of the Night Skies

Bats are by far the most important natural predators of night-flying insects, consuming great quantities of mosquitoes, moths, beetles, crickets, leafhoppers, chinch bugs, and a variety of aquatic insects. Many of these are serious crop pests, and others spread disease to humans or livestock.

A single little brown bat, one of North America's most abundant species, is capable of capturing 600 mosquitoes in an hour. One colony of 20 million Mexican free-tailed bats in central Texas eats up to half million pounds of insects *in a single night.*

How do they do this? Bats use their sophisticated sonar, called echolocation, to detect prey. Like dolphins, most bats communicate and navigate with these high-frequency sounds. Using echolocation alone, bats can "see" everything but color, and in total darkness can detect objects as fine as a human hair.

By consuming vast numbers of night-flying insects, bats form an integral link in ensuring environmental health. When bat populations are destroyed, insect pests can multiply, unchecked by their natural predators. The repercussions can be extremely harmful to humans.

For example, in Israel a campaign to eradicate fruit bats by poisoning their caves, instead killed almost 90% of the country's insectivorous bats. *Noctuid* moths, formerly controlled by the bats, proliferated and their caterpillars became major agricultural pests. To save crops, extensive chemical control is now required, in turn polluting the environment.

The loss of insectivorous bat populations leaves us increasingly dependent on pesticides, which already threaten our environmental and personal health. With over 850 million pounds of pesticides applied to America's crops each year, our groundwater is increasingly contaminated, and runoff is further damaging wildlife habitat in a chain of environmental degradation that must be reversed. Protecting bats is part of the solution.

Renewers of Rain Forests, Lifegivers to Deserts

Throughout tropical regions, fruit and nectar-eating bats are vital to the survival of rain forests, which in turn play an essential role in the stability of world climates. These forests, where more than 90% of all terrestrial plant and animal species live, contain our planet's richest biological diversity. But without bats to pollinate flowers or disperse seeds, the diversity of other rain forest animals and plants would be greatly reduced, threatening delicate balances with unknown consequences.

In West Africa, bats carry 90 to 98% of the seeds of "pioneer plants" that initiate forest regrowth on cleared land. These hardy trees and shrubs grow rapidly, soon attracting other mammals and birds that in turn bring seeds of different plants. Without bats, this cycle of rain forest regeneration might never begin.

Bats also play key roles in other tropical forests from Latin America to Asia and Australia. In the Pacific islands, as many as 40% of tree species depend on bats for seed dispersal or pollination, and further studies likely will reveal even more.

On the savannas of East Africa, the giant baobab is known as the "Tree of Life" because so many other plants and animals depend on it for their survival. But the tree itself depends on bats. Its showy white flowers open only at night and are specially adapted to be pollinated by bats. Without bats, the baobab could die out, triggering a chain of linked extinctions and threatening plant and animal life throughout the region.

In the Sonoran Desert of the southwestern United States and Mexico, long-nosed bats play a similarly critical role in the lives of several species of agaves (century plants) and giant cacti. As with Africa's baobab tree, the giant cacti provide food and shelter for countless other animals. The bats that pollinate their flowers and disperse their seeds were recently declared endangered; if they disappear, these majestic plants and the wildlife that rely on them, could be seriously threatened.

The relationships between plants and their animal pollinators and seed dispersers are the result of millions of years of evolutionary interplay. Ecologists

now know that even small disturbances can destroy entire systems of plant and animal life, and that it takes millions of additional years for species diversity to even begin recovery. Loss of plant and animal diversity is perhaps the most serious of long-term global problems we face.

Bats and Economics

Many of the world's most economically important plants rely on bats. Some crops from these plants are valued in the hundreds of millions of dollars each year and are crucial to the economies of cash-poor developing countries.

In Africa, rapidly declining flying foxes are the only known seed dispersers for the iroko tree, whose timber is worth millions of dollars annually. A recent study documented nearly 300 plant species in the Old World tropics alone that rely on bats. Some 450 commercial products come from these plants. Just one, the durian fruit of Southeast Asia, adds $120 million to local economies. Other products include medicines, food and beverages, timber, ornamentals, fiber and cordage, and dyes and tannins.

Many of our cultivated crop plants still rely on bats for their survival in the wild. These include fruits such as bananas, plantain, breadfruit, avocados, dates, figs, peaches, and mangoes. Other bat-dependent products are cloves, cashews, carob, balsa wood, kapok filler for life preservers, and tequila, which comes from agaves.

Although most of these plants are now commercially cultivated, wild ancestral stocks remain essential. They are the only source of genetic material for development of disease-resistant strains and for producing new, more productive plants in the future.

With many flying fox populations in jeopardy, the need to understand their vital ecological and economic roles is crucial.

People Need Bats

Bats affect our lives in more ways than we realize. Without bats, our grocery stores might not look the same, and mosquitoes would find the world a much safer place to live. Imagine an Arizona sunset without giant cacti

or the savannas of East Africa without baobab trees.

Even in places so hidden from humans that we are rarely aware of them, organisms that depend on bats for their survival are yielding treasures of great benefit to us. New species of bacteria discovered in American bat caves are now being studied by major corporations for use in chemical waste detoxification, gasohol

production, and improved detergents. Still others may soon be used in the production of new antibiotics.

When a colony of cave-dwelling bats is lost, the potential benefits of countless microorganisms and other animals perish with them. Some of these live in only one bat cave in all the world.

Loss of bats may seriously damage entire ecosystems upon which we ourselves depend. These losses are not reversible; the consequences are unpredictable and potentially disastrous.

The Need for Bat Conservation

The contributions bats make to the quality of life on earth and to the welfare of humans are many.

Yet humans are needlessly destroying bats nearly everywhere.

Bats are virtually defenseless, and large colonies make easy targets. A single act of vandalism can kill millions at a time, having a significant impact on the survival of an entire species. Many bats require large numbers for successful rearing of young, and most produce only one pup per year. These factors combine to make bats exceptionally vulnerable to extinction.

The Decline of Bats in Europe and North America

In Europe, bats that were common only 30 years ago are now endangered. In the United States, nearly 40% of our 43 bat species are on the endangered list or are official candidates for it. Vandalism and repeated disturbance in roosting caves is a primary cause.

Gray bats were among our most abundant animals at the turn of the century; now they are endangered. Indiana bats, also endangered, declined by 55% in less than 10 years.

In the early 1960s, Eagle Creek Cave in Arizona housed the world's largest known bat colony, approximately 30 million Mexican free-tailed bats. Yet they declined 99.9% in only six years. Imagine the local impact of more than a half million pounds of additional insects left uneaten each summer night.

The Plight of Flying Foxes and Other Tropical Bats

Some governments list bats as pests, targeting them for eradication. In Queensland, Australia, mass hunts have killed thousands of flying foxes at a time, even though many of Australia's most economically important timber trees rely on bats for pollination or seed dispersal. Flying fox numbers have declined drastically.

In Latin America, the common vampire bat, who feeds on blood, has proliferated with the arrival of humans who introduced livestock. In many places vampires now require control, but poorly trained government agents and local farmers often indiscriminately kill all bats, unaware that the majority of Latin America's 270 other bat species are highly beneficial.

Dawn bats, the primary pollinators of Southeast Asia's 120 million dollar durian crop, are declining rapidly from loss of cave roosts and uncontrolled harvest for human food.

Throughout Southeast Asia and the Pacific and Indian Ocean islands, flying fox populations are in jeopardy. On Guam, where bats are considered a delicacy, one of the island's two flying fox species recently became extinct without even being listed as endangered, and the second is now in serious trouble. Commercial export of flying foxes to Guam has decimated additional populations. Several species are now extinct from this and other unregulated hunting.

The Need is Urgent

The status of bats is so poorly known in most parts of the world that species are becoming extinct before they can be recognized as endangered. Even in the United States, we do not know the true status of some of our most widespread species.

Major ecosystem studies in tropical forests, where bats comprise almost half of all mammal species, have ignored bats as though they did not exist. Conservation planners, therefore, often fail to consider bats in projects to save tropical forests, even when the results of such neglect may seriously threaten their success.

In many places, once vast populations of bats now survive only as mere remnants. Many of the species needed in large numbers to maintain the balance of nature are, instead, at such low population levels that they are almost ecologically irrelevant.

For some it is too late, but for many others protective action now can save them.

Education is Essential

Bats are among the most intensely feared and relentlessly persecuted animals on earth. Through ignorance, many populations have been needlessly destroyed. Most people know little about bats, often believing popular myths. Changing these false perceptions is essential for lasting conservation progress.

TEST YOUR BAT Q

A. True or False?

_____1. Bats swoop down and become caught in people's hair.

_____2. Bats are the only kind of mammals that can fly.

_____3. Bats are flying mice.

_____4. Bats are blind.

_____5. Most bats are dirty and carry rabies.

_____6. If you see a bat on the ground during the day it might be sick.

_____7. There really are bats that feed on blood.

_____8. Bats produce several litters a year, just like mice.

_____9. Bats are ugly animals.

____10. A single bat can catch 600 mosquitoes in just one hour.

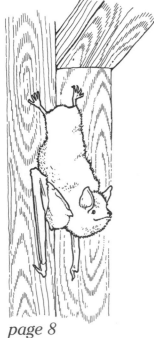

B. Bats around the world eat which of the following things:

*(Circle **all** correct answers.)*

fruit   nectar   insects   fish   blood

(Circle the correct answer to questions C through H.)

C. The biggest bat in the world has a wingspan of what size:

1 foot   3 feet   6 feet   50 feet

D. The smallest bat in the world is the size of what animal:

ant   mouse   guinea pig   bumblebee

E. Worldwide there are about_____ different species (kinds) of bats:

10   100   500   1,000

F. In the United States there are about_____ kinds of bats:

5   10   40   100

G. Bats are what kind of animals:

birds   reptiles   amphibians   mammals

H. Most bats produce _____ baby(ies) a year:

10   5   1   25

I. Bats are found in which of the following places:

*(Circle **all** correct answers.)*

tree holes   caves   attics   plant leaves
bridges   mines   tree bark   rock crevices

J. Bats live in which of the following kinds of areas:

*(Circle **all** correct answers.)*

mountains   deserts   rain forests   cities
prairies   wetlands   farmland   polar regions

K. Bats are important to the environment because they:

*(Circle **all** correct answers.)*

pollinate flowers   distribute plant seeds   eat insects

2 BAT ATTITUDES

Objective: *To correct common myths about bats*

Grades: *K-2*

Type of Activity: *Simple quiz and coloring*

Materials:
- *Copies of pages 11 and 12*
- *Crayons or markers*
- *Scissors*
- *Lamination material (optional)*

Background Information

Throughout history, bats have been shrouded in myth and superstition. Bats are shy, fly at night, and are difficult to observe. Hollywood has played a major role in perpetuating misinformation about these fascinating and highly beneficial animals.

On page 11 are six cartoons illustrating something that is true or false about bats. Make double-sided copies of pages 11 and 12 for each student. (Note that text on page 12 should line up with the appropriate cartoon.) Before looking at the answers on the reverse side, ask students to respond, true or false, to the statement on each cartoon. The individual cartoons can be colored and cut apart. Cartoons could later be laminated and used as a game for review. Children can also use the cards to quiz other students. The following provides additional information on each statement for educators to use when presenting the activity.

1. Bats Are Blind.
False.

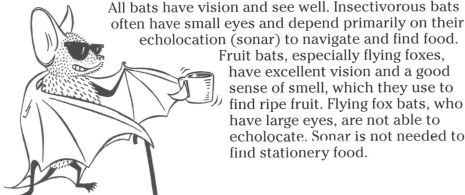

All bats have vision and see well. Insectivorous bats often have small eyes and depend primarily on their echolocation (sonar) to navigate and find food. Fruit bats, especially flying foxes, have excellent vision and a good sense of smell, which they use to find ripe fruit. Flying fox bats, who have large eyes, are not able to echolocate. Sonar is not needed to find stationery food.

2. Bats Get Caught in Your Hair.
False.

Insects often hover around people, and a hungry bat may seem to swoop down in hot pursuit of a pesky mosquito. Their sonar ability is sophisticated enough to find such an insect in complete darkness. They certainly are not going to blunder into a person's hair.

3. Bats Are Flying Mice.
False.

While bats may resemble mice with wings, they are not closely related to rodents. Both bats and mice are mammals, but studies indicate bats to be more closely related to primates (and humans) than to rodents. Flying foxes have a brain organization very similar to ours.

4. Bats Are Dirty and Many Carry Rabies.
False.

Bats are very clean and groom themselves several times a day just like cats. The issue of bats and rabies is greatly exaggerated. Bats can contract rabies just like all mammals, but they are not asymptomatic carriers of rabies, and they quickly die from the disease. The

incidence of rabies in bats is less than half of one percent. In more than 40 years of record-keeping in the U.S., only 20 people are believed to have died from contact with bats. As many or more people die *annually* from being attacked by their own pet dogs. People have little to fear from bats if they never try to handle them. An important message for children, especially when they come to like bats, is that bats are wild animals that should never be touched. Any bat or wild animal that can be approached is more likely than others to be sick.

5. Bats Are the Only Mammals That Can Truly Fly.
True.

Mammals such as flying squirrels are actually gliders. Bats are the only mammals capable of sustained flight. There is a great diversity of flight patterns among the nearly 1,000 kinds of bats. Some can hover like hummingbirds while feeding on nectar, and a few diurnal flying foxes are able to soar on thermals just like eagles.

6. Some Bats Can Catch up to 600 Mosquitoes in Just One Hour.
True.

The little brown bat, one of America's most common species, is capable of such a feat. On average, insectivorous bats eat about half their weight in insects each night. Nursing mothers sometimes eat more than their body weight. A Texas nursery colony of 20 million Mexican free-tailed bats can consume up to 500,000 pounds of insects in a single night.

True or False?

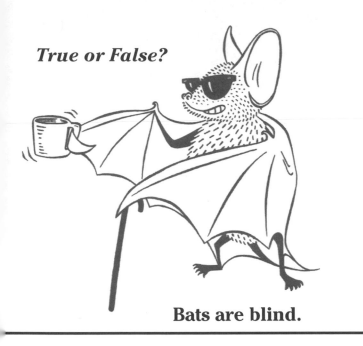

Bats are blind.

True or False?

Bats get
caught in your hair.

True or False?

Bats are flying mice.

True or False?

Bats
are dirty
and many
carry rabies.

True or False?

Bats are the only
mammals that truly fly.

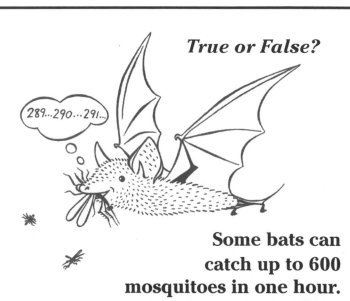

True or False?

Some bats can
catch up to 600
mosquitoes in one hour.

FALSE

Bats can find tiny insects in total darkness. They are much too smart to fly into people.

FALSE

No bats are blind and many can see very well. Insect-eating bats depend on sound and very good hearing to find food and get around in the dark.

FALSE

Bats are clean and groom themselves just like cats.

Bats can get rabies, like all mammals, but few do. Remember, bats are wild animals. You have nothing to fear if you never touch a bat.

FALSE

While both bats and mice are mammals, bats are not rodents and are more closely related to primates and people.

TRUE

Insect-eating bats can eat up to half their body weight in insects in one night. The record for mosquito catching is 600 in an hour!

TRUE

Some mammals, like flying squirrels, can glide. Bats are the only mammals that can really fly.

3 BAT CROSSWORD PUZZLES

Objective: *To introduce new words associated with bats*

Grades: *Puzzle A - 2-3*
Puzzle B - 3-5

Type of Activity: *Word game*

Materials:
• *Copies of page 14 or 15*
• *Pencils*

Background Information

To learn about bats, children need to become familiar with the terms used to describe their life style and habits. The following two crossword puzzles will familiarize children with basic bat terminology. The puzzles differ in degree of difficulty. The answers are included in a box on each page. The teacher may choose to cover these when copying the puzzles.

Answer Key

Puzzle A

Across
1. Bats are the only kind of mammal that can **fly**.
2. An animal that is disappearing is said to be **endangered**.
3. Most mother bats produce only **one** (how many) baby each year.
4. A bat is a **mammal**.
5. Most bats are active only at **night**.
6. Many bats use **sound** to navigate and find food.

Down
1. Most bats in the world eat **insects**.
2. **Bats** are the only mammals that truly fly.
3. A baby bat is called a **pup**.
4. A bat's wing is very similar to our own **hand**.
5. All bats can see, no bats are **blind**.
6. Many bats spend at least part of the year living in **caves**.

Puzzle B (more advanced)

Across
1. An animal that is active at night is called **nocturnal**.
2. All bats can see; no bats are **blind**.
3. The scientific name for bats, which means hand-wing, is **chiroptera**.
4. A kind of bat whose face looks like a dog is a flying **fox**.
5. A bat that feeds on insects is called **insectivorous**.
6. Most mother bats produce only **one** (how many) baby a year.
7. Many bats spend part of the year living in **caves**.
8. Echolocation used by bats is a kind of **sonar**.

Down
1. The process of navigating and locating food using sound is called **echolocation**.
2. A bat is a **mammal**.
3. Nectar bats **pollinate** flowers, just like hummingbirds.
4. An animal that is disappearing is said to be **endangered**.
5. There are nearly a **thousand** (how many) kinds of bats.
6. A baby bat is called a **pup**.
7. About 70% of all bats eat **insects**.
8. A group of bats living together is called a **colony**.

BAT CROSSWORD PUZZLE A

Across

1. Bats are the only kind of mammal that can _____.
2. An animal that is disappearing is said to be _____.
3. Most mother bats produce only _____ (how many) baby each year.
4. A bat is a _____.
5. Most bats are active only at _____.
6. Many bats use _____ to navigate and find food.

Down

1. Most bats in the world eat _____.
2. _____ are the only kind of mammals that truly fly.
3. A baby bat is called a _____.
4. A bat's wing is very similar to our own _____.
5. All bats can see; no bats are _____.
6. Many bats spend at least part of the year living in _____.

Answers
caves
sound
blind
night
hand
mammal
one
pup
endangered
bats
fly
insects

BAT CROSSWORD PUZZLE B

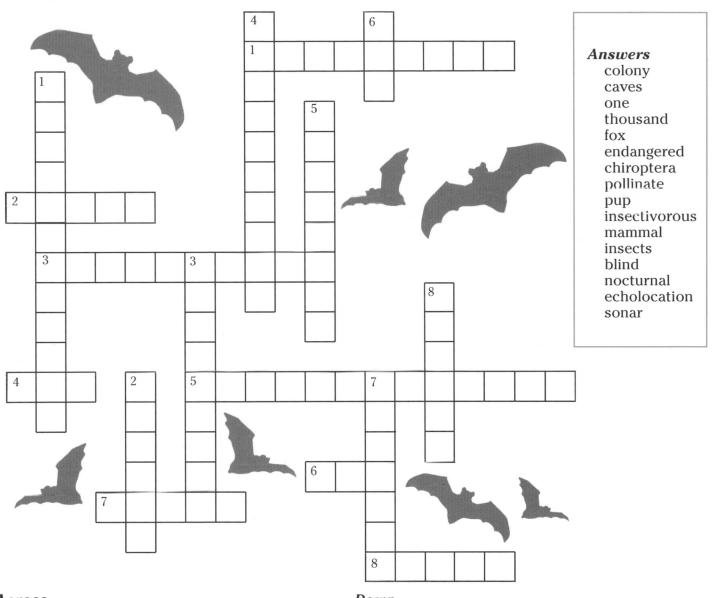

Answers
colony
caves
one
thousand
fox
endangered
chiroptera
pollinate
pup
insectivorous
mammal
insects
blind
nocturnal
echolocation
sonar

Across
1. An animal that is active at night is called
   _____.
2. All bats can see; no bats are _____.
3. The scientific name for bats, which means hand-wing, is _____.
4. The kind of bat whose face looks like a dog is a flying _____.
5. A bat that feeds on insects is called _____.
6. Most mother bats produce _____ (how many) baby a year.
7. Many bats spend part of the year living in _____.
8. Echolocation used by bats is a kind of _____.

Down
1. The process of navigating and locating food using sound is called _____.
2. A bat is a _____.
3. Nectar bats _____ flowers, just like hummingbirds.
4. An animal that is disappearing is said to be _____.
5. There are nearly a _____ (how many) kinds of bats.
6. A baby bat is called a _____.
7. About 70% of all bats eat _____.
8. A group of bats living together is called a _____.

4 SEEING WITH YOUR EARS

Objective: *To understand how bats use sound to navigate and find food in the dark*

Grades: *3-5*

Type of Activity: *Demonstration and discussion*

Materials:
- *Basketballs or similar sized bouncing balls*
- *Blindfolds*
- *Ear plugs or cotton balls*

Background Information

Even though no bats are blind, some 70% use a sonar system, called echolocation, to navigate in the dark and find food. They can detect the size, texture, even the direction of a moving insect, using sound alone. Bats emit sound pulses, produced in the larynx, through the mouth or nose. As these sounds come in contact with objects—trees, buildings, or potential food— they are reflected back as echoes and collected by the bat's ears. Information contained in the echoes is processed in the bat's brain instantaneously, enabling the bat to fly rapidly through a cluttered environment without a collision. Most of these sound pulses are produced at a frequency too high for humans to hear without the aid of special equipment. Instruments, called bat detectors, render the calls audible to the human hearing range enabling people to listen in on the hunt. Using special equipment, scientists can now identify many species of bats who use certain frequencies and characteristic patterns, in the same

manner that we can identify bird songs.

For many years, scientists were puzzled about how bats were able to navigate in the dark. In the late 1700s, an Italian naturalist and priest, Lazzaro Spallanzani, made the first attempt to understand the mystery of bat navigation. He put an owl and a bat in a semi-dark room and found both could fly quite well in low light. In complete darkness, the owl was helpless and bumped into everything, but the bat did not. He then put a small hood over the bat's head. With its head covered, the bat too became helpless. Later, Spallanzani reviewed additional experiments by Swiss surgeon Louis Jurine. With renewed interest, he took his research a step

further. When placing brass tubes in a bat's ears, he found that its sense of direction totally failed if the tubes were plugged. But it wasn't until about 1938 that Harvard scientist Donald Griffin, with the aid of special recording equipment, learned that bats navigate by transmitting high frequency sound pulses through their mouths and then collect the echoes with their ears.

Not all bats use echolocation. Flying fox bats, from the suborder Megachiroptera (see Activity 8), have very good eyesight and an excellent sense of smell to find food in the dark. They feed on fruit, pollen, and nectar and don't need a sophisticated sonar system to chase darting insects. Almost without exception, they usually roost out in the open and

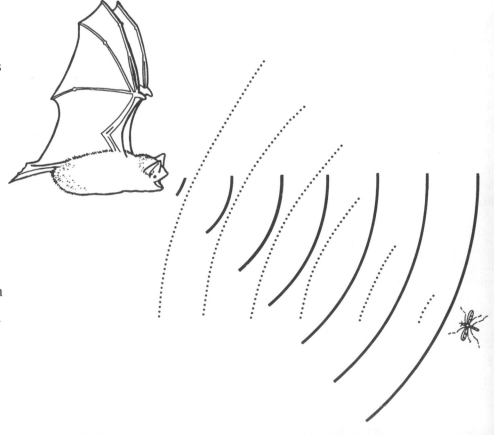

not deep in dark places like caves. Hence, flying foxes typically have very large eyes and small ears.

Many children are familiar with some aspects of echolocation. Most have had some experience generating echoes in canyons or among tall buildings. In this exercise a ball will be used to simulate a sound wave.

Divide the class into pairs in a gymnasium or other large empty room. Each pair gets a large bouncing ball. They need to use two walls and should stand closer to one wall than the other. Each taking a turn, they will throw the ball (sound wave) towards the wall. As the sound wave (ball) hits the wall, it (the echo) will bounce back. As the thrower *sees* the ball returning he/she points and follows it with a finger as it returns. The partner retrieves the ball. Each partner takes a turn at both the close and far walls. Point out to the students that the ball (echo) returns more quickly from the closer wall.

The second part of the exercise enables each pair to do the exercise like bats. One partner is blindfolded. The other partner orients the blindfolded partner toward the wall and hands him/her the ball to throw. Both partners get a chance to throw against the close wall and far wall, again pointing to the ball (echo) and following it with a finger as it returns. Each student should be able to determine, from hearing alone, which is the close wall and which one is far and indicate the direction in which the ball is moving.

For the third part of the exercise, in addition to the blindfold, the partners will also use a pair of ear plugs, or alternative means of blocking hearing, and repeat the same exercise on the near and far walls. Could the student identify the near and far walls, and could he/she follow the track of the echo (bouncing ball) with a finger? The students should now have a better appreciation of how important echolocation is to navigate in darkness.

Following this indoor exercise, take the class outside for a short hike and discussion. Outside, several questions can be asked. What kinds of obstacles must a bat avoid while it hunts for insects at night? (Buildings, trees, rocks, power lines, moving cars.) Using examples the children can see, ask how the bat knows what is closer, the tree 10 feet away, or the building 100 feet away. (Sound waves return faster if the obstacle is closer.) How does a bat remember where all those obstacles are while it chases a darting insect? (The brain processes and remembers all the information while the bat flies.) What happens if it rains or gets very windy? (Bats may have to stop hunting until the weather improves.) What happens if two bats are chasing the same insect? (First come, first served!) What other kinds of animals hunt for flying insects at night? (Not many. That's why bats hunt at night; they don't have to compete for food with animals like birds.)

5 CLOSE ENCOUNTER WITH A BAT

Objective: *To teach children what to do when encountering a grounded bat*

Grades: *1-5*

Type of Activity: *A one-act play*

Materials:
- *Copies of script, pages 19 and 20*
- *Jackets*
- *Bookbags*
- *Glove*
- *Rubber bat*
- *Pile of leaves*

Background Information

While bats are fascinating, gentle, and frequently very attractive animals, one drawback to their increase in popularity is that children may want to keep them as pets or pick up a bat they find on the ground. Bats are wild animals and one important role played by educators is to teach kids that no wild animal, including bats, should ever be touched. Bats that can be easily approached are more likely than others to be sick. People need not be afraid if they never try to handle bats. Should a child encounter a bat on the ground, he/she should never touch it, but rather call an adult to come and remove it so it will not be found by others.

Bat Conservation International does not recommend keeping bats as pets. Insectivorous bats have very specific dietary requirements including large quantities of a variety of insects. Few do well in captivity. Only experienced animal handlers who have the pre-exposure rabies vac-

cinations should handle bats or other wild mammals. While the incidence of rabies in bats is very low (less than half of one percent in the U.S.), it is not worth taking a chance.

The following play will teach children how to behave when finding a sick or injured bat on the ground. Following the production, engage the class in a discussion emphasizing the main points:

1. Never touch a wild bat, and
2. Call an adult to remove a grounded bat to a safe place.

The play can be performed by five children and one adult (or older student).

CLOSE ENCOUNTER WITH A BAT

CHARACTERS: Meagan, Sarah, Mrs. Johnson, Jeffrey, Carlos, and Ryan

(A group of children are walking home from school carrying jackets and bookbags, singing the school song. Suddenly, a boy bringing up the rear — Carlos — stops and bends down to look at something on the ground. The others stop, turn around, and make a circle around the object on the ground.)

MEAGAN	What is it?
JEFFREY	It's a dead bird.
SARAH	No it isn't! It doesn't have any feathers.
CARLOS	It's a bat!
RYAN	Ick...Be careful, it will suck your blood.
SARAH	You're crazy, Ryan, bats around here don't eat blood. We studied bats in school. This one looks like a little brown bat.
JEFFREY	Is it alive?
MEAGAN	I think so, but it's not moving much.
CARLOS	I'm gonna pick it up and take it home.
SARAH	No! Don't touch it. It might be sick. Our teacher told us never to touch bats, especially those that are on the ground and can't fly.
RYAN	Well, what should we do?
MEAGAN	I'm gonna get my mom. She likes bats. She'll know what to do.
	(Meagan runs off stage.)
RYAN	Gee, it's really small. I thought bats were big and had huge fangs dripping with blood.
SARAH	Ryan, you've been watching too many horror movies.
JEFFREY	Well, I think it's cute. I'm sorry that it's sick.

(Enter Meagan and her mother, Mrs. Johnson. Mrs. Johnson bends down and takes a careful look. She pulls a leather glove out of her pocket, slips it on and gently picks up the bat.)

MRS. JOHNSON	Yes, it's a little brown bat, probably not quite full grown.
MEAGAN	Is it alive?
MRS. JOHNSON	No honey, I'm afraid it's dead.
EVERYONE	Aw.
JEFFREY	Poor little bat.
RYAN	Can I touch it?
EVERYONE	Yeah, can we touch it?
MRS. JOHNSON	No, we don't know whether the bat was sick or died from an injury. Remember, this is a wild animal. Are we supposed to touch wild animals?
EVERYONE	Nooo.

MRS. JOHNSON	But let's look at him a minute. See his soft brown fur. Can anyone tell me what kind of animal he is?
RYAN	He's a flying mouse!
EVERYONE	*(Laughs)*
MRS. JOHNSON	Well, that's not exactly right. He's a mammal, just like a dog or cat, but he's not a mouse. In fact, bats are more closely related to people than to mice.
MRS. JOHNSON	Look at his wing. *(Holding up her hand)* Did you know that the bones in his wing are actually fingers? A bat flies with its hands. *(Motioning her hand like a wing)*
SARAH	Bats are pretty neat.
RYAN	Does he suck blood?
EVERYONE	*(Shouts)* No!!
MRS. JOHNSON	No, he eats insects. Would you believe that just one little bat like this can catch up to 600 mosquitoes in just one hour?
CARLOS	Wow, I wish we had more bats at my house. The mosquitoes are terrible.
MRS. JOHNSON	Yes, unfortunately bats are declining all over the world. Most people don't know how important they are and kill them. When I was a little girl, there were many more bats than there are today.
SARAH	What are you going to do with that bat, Mrs. Johnson?
MRS. JOHNSON	We need to take him away so somebody doesn't come along and pick him up. What did we say about wild animals?
EVERYONE	Don't touch them.
MRS. JOHNSON	I think we should bury him. Let's go over to those trees.
	(Mrs. Johnson digs a small hole, lays the bat inside and then covers up the hole with leaves.)
MEAGAN	Poor little bat.
SARAH	I wish we could have saved him.
MRS. JOHNSON	I know, it is sad isn't it? But you can help other bats by just appreciating them and telling your friends what you've learned today. Bats need lots of friends.
	(Mrs. Johnson takes Meagan by the hand.)
MRS. JOHNSON	Well, children, you'd better all go home now. It's late and your parents will worry.
	(Walks off stage with Meagan)
EVERYONE	Goodbye Mrs. Johnson; goodbye Meagan. *(Start walking off stage)*
CARLOS	Gee, I don't feel like singing anymore.
SARAH	Me neither.
RYAN	Hey! Maybe we could start a bat club.
JEFFREY	That's a great idea. Then we could learn a lot more about bats. We can ask the science teacher in the morning.
	(Chatter continues as kids move off stage)

6 GOING, GOING, GONE

Objective: *To understand the reasons for bat decline, endangerment and extinction*

Grades: *2-5*

Type of Activity: *Lecture and discussion followed by coloring*

Materials:
- *Copies of pages 23 and 24*
- *Crayons or markers*

Background Information

Bats are in decline nearly everywhere they are found. In the U.S., almost 40% of bat species are endangered or are candidates for such status. In some parts of the world bats have gone extinct before they could even be declared endangered. This activity deals with the causes of bat decline. After presenting the background material to the students, lead a discussion about what kinds and combinations of threats there are to bats in the immediate area. Ask the children to think about what they can do to help protect local bats. Following the discussion, give each child a double-sided copy of pages 23 and 24 which feature four threatened or endangered bats in the U.S. Be sure the text on the back side lines up with the appropriate bat. The page can be colored and displayed.

Ignorance, Myth, and Superstition

Bats have suffered from centuries of myth and superstition. What are some of the myths? (See Activity 2). This misinformation has been exaggerated by Hollywood films. The shy nature of bats has also helped perpetuate misunderstanding. Bats fly at night and are difficult to become acquainted with—the main reason that education is key to their conservation. When people destroy bats they usually act out of ignorance. Unfortunately, ignorance leads to the destruction of millions of harmless and highly beneficial bats each year. Many people believe that they are doing the world a favor when they kill bats. They couldn't be more wrong. Fortunately, once people learn the facts about bats, most are quite willing to accept them as a beneficial part of nature. Many "converts" become active friends of bats and help others to learn about how important bats are to the environment.

Habitat Loss

Habitat loss is another major reason for bat decline. Habitat is that area an animal needs to "make a living." It's the space where an animal sleeps and finds food. For some bats, that can be a very large area. As more and more wild land is developed for human living space, plants and animals must try to live with less. With the loss of forests, bats have lost food and roosting space in trees. For example, a mixed hardwood forest is home to a great variety of insects on which bats will feed. If the forest is replaced with a hundred acres of corn, the diversity of insects is dramatically reduced. There will not be a continual variety of hatching insects, so the bats must leave or starve. Most bats are adapted to specific habitats in which to live and find food. They simply cannot move to a different kind of place and learn to eat new food. Many kinds of bats live at least part of the year in caves where they have very specific temperature and humidity requirements. Throughout the world their cave roosts are being destroyed or altered. If they lose their traditional roosting space, it may be impossible to find a new place to live. With disappearing rain forests and other habitat, many animals cannot adapt and are headed toward extinction.

Roosting Habits

Many kinds of bats roost together in large numbers. Baby bats of some species roost in densities of up to 500 per square foot. Packing tightly together helps these small mammals stay warm. Some colonies in the U.S. contain millions of individuals. Unfortunately, when bats are together in large numbers they are extremely vulnerable to disturbance. A single vandalous act can kill millions in a matter of minutes.

Human Disturbance

A major cause of bat decline is intentional human disturbance. Many bat caves have been vandalized by people seeking to kill bats. Many such people are simply uninformed about the value of bats. But the reverse is also true. Some people unknowingly disturb bats when they only want to see and appreciate them. They enter caves when the bats are hibernating in winter or raising young in early summer. If bats are disturbed during hibernation they may wake up, fly around, and waste precious body fat needed to keep them alive until spring. Too much disturbance will cause the bats to starve. Most U.S. bats give birth in early June. Disturbance of maternity colonies may cause the mothers to drop or abandon their young, or move to cooler roosts where fewer survive. Many conservation groups are now posting signs at important bat caves to keep people out during critical times of the year. Some very special caves are fitted with gates to keep people out, guaranteeing bats the peace and quiet they need.

Slow Rate of Reproduction

For their size, bats are some of the slowest reproducing animals. While mice and rats produce several large litters of young each year, most bats produce only one baby per year. If a colony suffers some kind of disaster, natural or otherwise, recovery is very slow. Repeated catastrophes or a combination of threats can, over a short time, push a species to extinction.

Pesticide Poisoning

Pesticide poisoning causes problems for many kinds of animals. As agriculture has grown, so has the use of pesticides. In the course of treating crops with poisons, insects eat or become covered with chemicals. Animals, such as bats, later feed on these insects and ingest the toxins. The chemicals are stored in a bat's body fat. When the bat burns up this fat during migration or hibernation, the chemicals are re-

leased and the bat dies. Studies at national animal health laboratories have shown that this is a serious problem for bats in parts of the U.S. as well as in many foreign countries where pesticides are less regulated.

Human Consumption

In many parts of the world, such as the Pacific islands and Southeast Asia, flying fox bats are eaten as food. With the arrival of firearms, freezers, and flight service between islands, bats have been hunted, stored and shipped to other countries. Because most of these bats produce only a single baby per year, populations cannot sustain unregulated harvest and many species have declined, with few left. On some islands, bats pollinate or disperse the seeds for up to 40% of the forest trees, making them extremely valuable to the people who live there. Several species have already gone extinct. New legislation now prohibits the international sale of many kinds of flying fox fruit bats.

Migratory Species

Many animals migrate to different places when food and water become scarce. Bats that migrate can suffer from all the above threats in at least two different places. For example, several species of southern U.S. bats migrate to Mexico where there is abundant food in winter. They are vulnerable to disturbance and pesticide poisoning at both the summer and winter roosts as well as in the places they stop to rest while traveling. Migratory birds face many of the same kinds of threats.

***Eumops perotis*, Western Mastiff Bat**

***Leptonycteris curasoae*,
Lesser Long-nosed Bat**

***Myotis grisescens*, Gray Bat**

***Plecotus townsendii*,
Townsend's Big-eared Bat**

Leptonycteris curasoae, Lesser Long-nosed Bat

Many desert plants, including saguaro and organpipe cacti, and 60 or more kinds of agave plants, rely on this reddish-brown nectar bat for pollination. It is endangered because many of its cave roosts have been disturbed or destroyed. Decline of long-nosed bats threatens the survival not only of plants they pollinate, but also of animals that require these plants for food and shelter.

Eumops perotis, Western Mastiff Bat

Almost nothing is known about mastiff bats. They are no longer found in many previously occupied roosts and are now candidates for endangered status. This is the largest bat found in the U.S., with a wingspan of nearly two feet. These dark gray bats roost in cliff faces in the Southwest and feed high above the ground.

Plecotus townsendii, Townsend's Big-eared Bat

Huge ears assist this tan-colored endangered bat in finding moths to eat. When sleeping, the bat's ears are coiled and look like ram's horns. The base of the ear is crinkled similar to an accordion. Because the bat lives in the entrances of caves, it has suffered greatly from human disturbance.

Myotis grisescens, Gray Bat

The endangered gray bat spends most of its life in caves. Human disturbance in its cave roosts led to a severe decline, and the species was declared endangered. With protection, it is now increasing in numbers. This southeastern bat can eat as many as 3,000 insects in one night.

7 BAT MASKS

Objective: *To introduce bat diversity and explain significance of facial anatomy*

Grades: *K-5*

Type of Activity: *Craft project*

Materials:
- *Copies of pages 26, 27, 28, and 29 on white card stock*
- *Crayons or colored markers*
- *Scissors*
- *Hole punch*
- *String elastic*

Background Information

Certainly one of the most fascinating aspects of bats is their facial anatomy. The great diversity of face types is due to the differences in life style and diet. For example, some bats that feed on nectar need long, thin faces to insert into flowers, while insectivorous bats have shorter muzzles and stronger jaws to chomp down on insects.

The bat masks will give children an opportunity to examine the facial anatomy of four different kinds of bats. Copy the masks on card stock paper, trim excess, punch holes on both sides, and attach elastic. Children can use their imaginations when coloring the masks. Encourage children to talk about the differences they see and why a bat might need big eyes (to see in the dark), big ears or a funny looking nose (both part of very sophisticated echolocation systems). (See Activity 4 for a more thorough discussion of echolocation.) The following provides information about the four bats so that the educator can lead a discussion on the interesting features of each species.

Lonchorhina aurita, Sword-nosed Bat

Huge ears, nose-leaf (a leaf-shaped projection of skin above the nose), and other facial flaps are part of this bat's complicated echolocation system. The bat's nose-leaf is the largest of any species. It is thought that the nose-leaf helps direct sound being emitted through the nose. It feeds on insects in dense foliage where extra-large ears and a nose-leaf help the bat to find food. This insectivorous bat is rarely seen and scientists know little about it. It lives in Latin America.

Rhinolophus yunanensis, Dobson's Horseshoe Bat

Big ears and strange-looking facial flaps are all part of one of the world's most sophisticated navigational systems. To scientists who understand the bat's special adaptations, even a face like this is beautiful. This Asian bat emits pulses through the nose, and the facial flaps may aid in sound delivery when navigating or hunting insects. Big ears capture echoes bouncing off objects.

Pteropus poliocephalus, Grey-headed Flying Fox

A large bat with a wingspan of more than four feet, it feeds only on fruit and nectar and is an important pollinator of several kinds of Australian timber trees. Not able to echolocate (note small ears), this flying fox has excellent vision (note large eyes) and a good sense of smell to find ripe fruit. It is called a flying fox due to its facial resemblance to a fox.

Macrotus californicus, California Leaf-nosed Bat

This bat snatches moths and other insects from foliage or the ground as it flies above the desert floor. It has larger eyes than most insectivorous bats. Its huge ears, which give it excellent hearing, enable it to detect even the footsteps of walking insects. The California leaf-nosed bat lives in the western U.S. and Mexico.

Lonchorhina aurita, Sword-nosed Bat

***Rhinolophus yunanensis*, Dobson's Horseshoe Bat**

Pteropus poliocephalus, Grey-headed Flying Fox

***Macrotus californicus*, California Leaf-nosed Bat**

GREETINGS FROM A BAT

Objective: *To introduce the scientific classification system for bats*

Grades: *K-5*

Type of Activity: *Craft project*

Materials:
- *Copies of pages 31 and 32 on heavy colored paper or card stock*
- *Crayons or markers*
- *Scissors*
- *Envelopes (optional)*

Background Information

For grades K-5, the teacher can bypass the section on creating a scientific classification for the two bat species, and give a simpler introduction on the differences between mega and micro bats.

All forms of life known to science are classified and given a scientific name, and many have a common name too. To classify living (and fossil) organisms, scientists use a system like the one shown here. (There are additional subcategories available that aren't used in this exercise). This system makes it possible to generalize a lot of information about the organism. In progressing downward from kingdom to species, there is an increase in detail.

The example included is for *Myotis evotis*, one of the bats featured in the greeting card activity found on pages 31 and 32. Copy the classification scheme, in order, on a blackboard or on a large piece of paper so that it can be viewed by all students. The classification names for the second bat, *Eidolon helvum*, in the card

design are listed separately. Make a second list of categories, post the accompanying names, and ask the students to place each name in the appropriate category. Write the second scheme alongside the first example. Following this brief exercise, children can begin the accompanying craft project described at the end of this activity.
(text continued on page 33)

Classification scheme for the micro bat, *Myotis evotis*.

Kindgom: Animalia
Five kingdoms are recognized. The two most familiar are Animalia, (animals), and Plantae, (plants)

Phyllum: Chordata
Animals with a dorsal hollow nerve chord, or more simply, a nerve chord down the back.

Subphyllum: Vertebrata
This Subphyllum contains all animals with the spinal chord enclosed in a vertebral column. (Examples: Fish, frogs, snakes, birds, dogs, and people all have a backbone.)

Class: Mammalia
Includes all mammals, animals that have fur or hair, bear live young, and nurse offspring with milk.

Order: Chiroptera
All bats, the only mammals that truly fly. The name means hand-wing.

Suborder: Microchiroptera
The group of generally small, mostly insectivorous (micro) bats, all of which have the ability to echolocate. They are found throughout the world.

Family: Vespertilionidae
Most common family of bats from which come many U.S. species. Many live in caves, capture insects in flight, and have a characteristic tooth pattern. Family names always end in ae.

Genus: *Myotis*
The genus is the first part of an organism's scientific name. *Myotis* means mouse-eared. The first letter of a genus is always capitalized, and the word underlined or italicized.

Species: *evotis*
The species is the second part of a scientific name. The word *evotis* means big-eared. All letters in the name are lower-case and the word underlined or italicized.

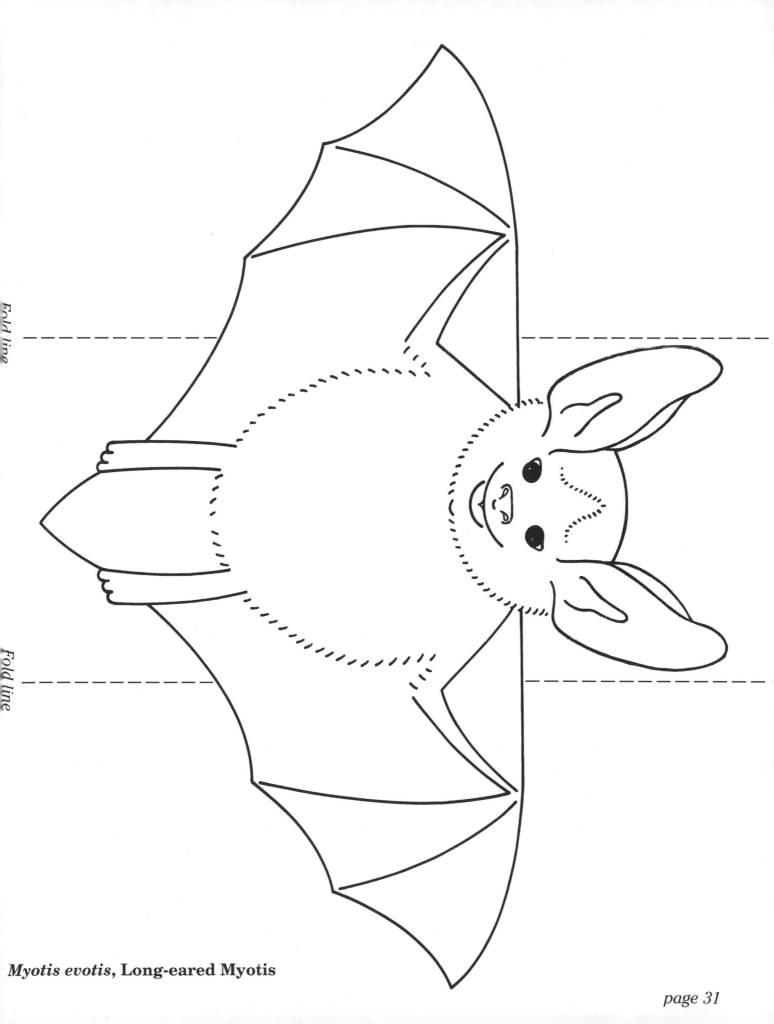

Fold line

Fold line

Myotis evotis, **Long-eared Myotis**

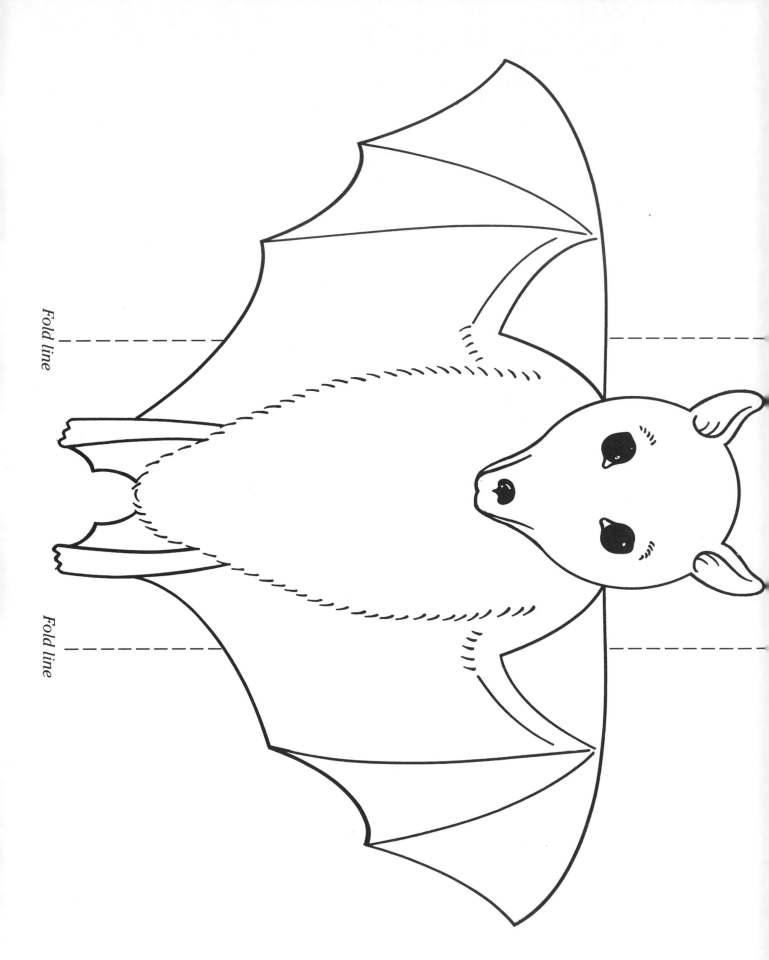

Fold line

Fold line

***Eidolon helvum,* Straw-colored Flying Fox**

page 32

All organisms have a two-part scientific name, for example *Myotis evotis*. The scientific name for humans is *Homo sapiens* and means wise man. No two kinds can have exactly the same name. The common name for this bat is long-eared myotis.

The following are names for the Classification Scheme of a Megachiropteran (mega) bat, *Eidolon helvum*, the straw-colored flying fox. List the categories (words in bold) in proper order on the blackboard. Present the corresponding names in random order, and ask students to place the correct name in each category.

Kingdom: Animalia
Phyllum: Chordata
Subphyllum: Vertebrata
Class: Mammalia
Order: Chiroptera
Suborder: Megachiroptera
    With one exception do not echolocate; feed on fruit, nectar and pollen; and are found only in the Old World tropics—Africa, Asia, Australia, and on many islands in the Pacific.
Family: Pteropodidae
    The family that includes all flying foxes.
Genus: *Eidolon*
    Means "phantom."
Species: *helvum*
    Means "pale yellow."

Mega Bats and Micro Bats

As seen in the classification schemes, the scientific order for bats is called Chiroptera, meaning hand-wing, and the order is further broken into two suborders, Microchiroptera and Megachiroptera. The two designs for bat greeting cards on pages 31 and 32 feature examples of the two distinct kinds of bats, a representative insectivorous micro bat, and a flying fox, called a mega bat. Micro bats tend to be small, many weighing less than half an ounce. Most eat insects and they all echolocate to navigate and find food. Mega bats are generally quite large, many having wingspans from three to nearly six feet, and often have dog-like faces. They feed only on fruit, nectar and pollen, which they find using excellent eyesight and a good sense of smell. Only one species in nearly 200 has a rudimentary form of echolocation.

While children make the cards, encourage them to talk about some of the obvious differences in the two bat faces. For example, ask them to think about why one needs big ears (for echolocation) and another big eyes (to see ripe fruit in trees).

Copy the designs from pages 31 and 32 on heavy white paper or card stock. Students can color each card or, for a quicker activity, the designs can be copied on colored paper. Trim off the excess paper and fold according to the instructions. This is a great Halloween activity. Each card can contain a message or poem of the child's own choosing.

9 BAT CAVE BULLETIN BOARD

Objective: *To become familiar with bat anatomy and learn why many bats live in caves*

Grades: *K-5*

Type of Activity: *Construct a bat cave*

Materials:
- *Double-sided copies of pages 35 and 36 on heavy tan or brown paper*
- *Kraft paper or sheets of plain newsprint*
- *Tacks and staples*
- *Tape*
- *Scissors*

Background Information

A bat actually flies with its fingers. Refer to the anatomy diagram on page 37. Have the children compare their own hands with the bat. Locate the thumb and four fingers, which are the wing bones. The bat's upper arm, forearm and fingers are similar to ours but of different proportions. In addition, they are connected by an expanded membrane to complete a wing flight surface. Examine the other parts of the bat — eyes, ears, nose, hind legs. Discuss some of the differences between this bat and people. Large eyes see better in the dark, and a short neck helps to concentrate body weight and center of gravity. Bats don't walk on their hind feet, and they have short legs adapted for attaching to roosting surfaces.

About half of the bats in the United States live in caves for at least part of the year. In many ways this is a safe place to live. The temperature and humidity are relatively stable, it affords protection from weather, and few predators can harm bats while they are sleeping. By hanging upside down by their claws, bats can utilize spaces many other animals cannot. Also, hanging upside down is an easy position from which to take flight rapidly.

Many bats spend the winter hibernating in caves, relying on stored body fat for energy. Disturbance to bats during hibernation can cause them to burn up fat that is needed to keep them alive until spring. In the summer, many bats raise their young in caves. Disturbance to maternity caves in May, June, and July can cause mothers to drop or abandon young. Children should be taught not to disturb bats in caves.

The bat cave bulletin board is a wonderful activity for the month of October or during a study unit on bats. Construct the cave area by first lining the bulletin board space with wrapping paper, then crumpling up large sheets of paper or newsprint to simulate rock. Paper can be mounted to the bulletin board with tape and staples.

Give each child in the class a double-sided copy of pages 35 and 36 and have them cut out the bat figure and fold the wings according to the diagram. Also using the diagram, the teacher can explain simple bat anatomy and the children can compare the bat to themselves. Each child can attach his/her own bat to the cave.

In the empty spaces around the bats, the students can write in facts they have learned about bats or attach drawings, poems and essays. Before the exhibit is removed, other classes can be invited to view the bat cave and learn from what the students have assembled. A variation on this bulletin board cave is to create a similar cave inside a large appliance box.

BATS SLEEP DURING THE DAY

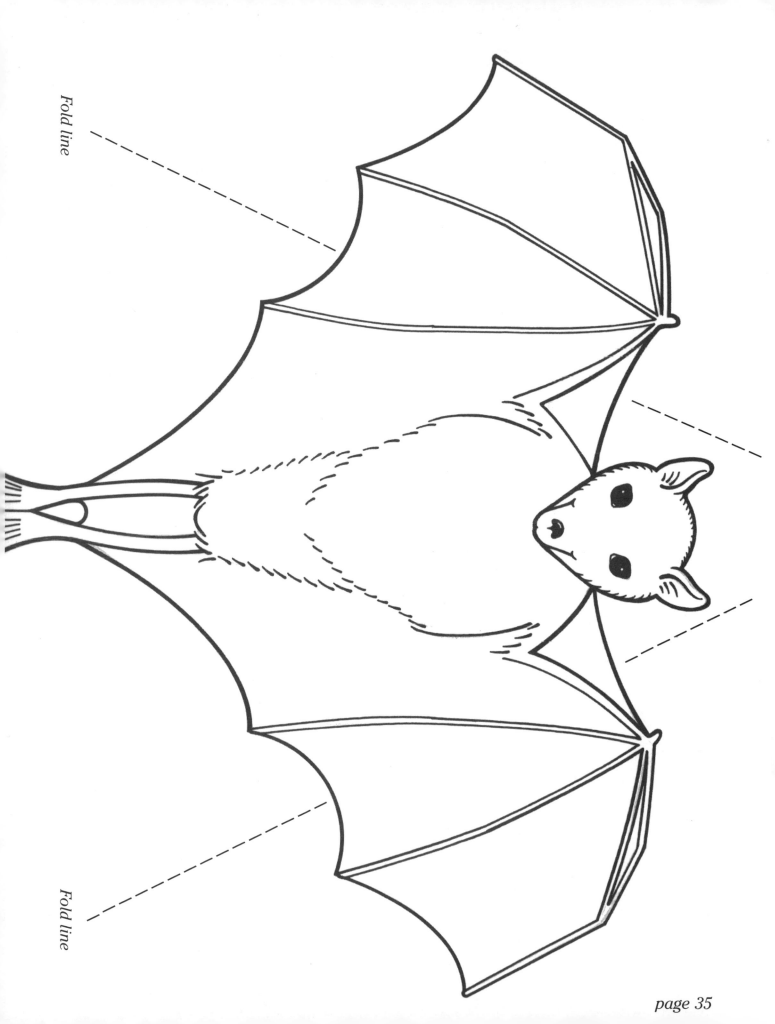

Fold line

Fold line

Fold line

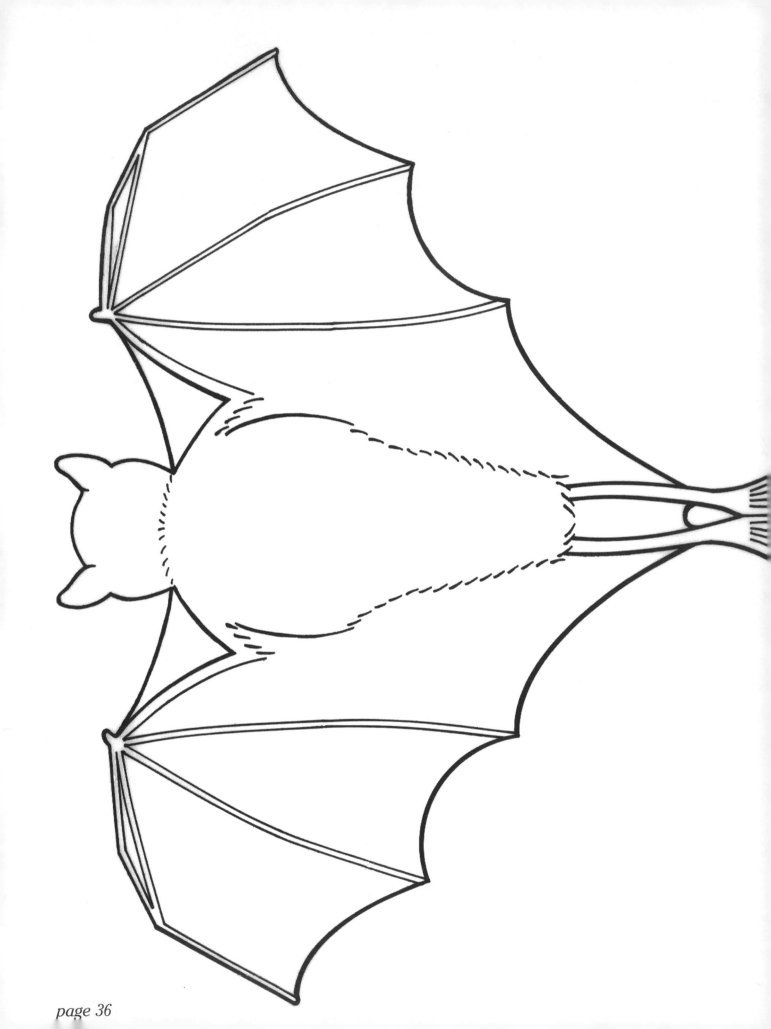

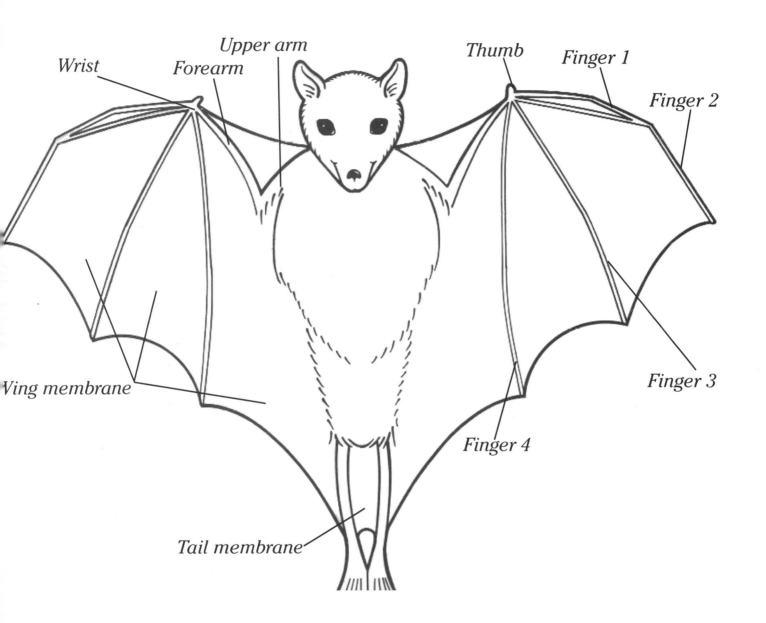

Wrist

Upper arm

Forearm

Thumb

Finger 1

Finger 2

Wing membrane

Finger 3

Finger 4

Tail membrane

Anatomy of a Bat

10 WHAT'S FOR DINNER?

Objective: *To familiarize students with the variety of bat diets*

Grades: *K-3*

Type of Activity: *Mobile craft project*

Materials:
- *Copies of pages 39, 40, and 41*
- *Crayons or markers*
- *Glue*
- *Scissors*
- *Large embroidery needle (or hole puncher)*
- *Heavy-duty black thread*
- *Two plastic straws per student (or a coat hanger)*

Background Information

The nearly 1,000 different kinds of bats in the world eat a variety of food items. The diversity of diets is not only interesting, but what and how bats eat is vital to ecosystems as diverse as rain forests and deserts.

Give each child copies of pages 39, 40, and 41. After coloring the bats and food items, students cut them out and attach the food item nearest the bat as indicated by the mobile diagram. Glue the pieces together. Holes are then made with the needle, and thread is attached to each bat. The five bats with thread are tied to the straws as shown in the diagram and then adjusted so they balance. The following provides information for each kind of bat featured.

Bats That Eat Nectar (nectarivory)

Throughout the world's tropics and subtropics, many kinds of bats feed on nectar and pollen and serve as pollinators for a variety of trees and shrubs. Bats are especially important in rain forests where their pollination activities help maintain the diversity of plant life. When a bat inserts its head into a flower to obtain nectar, its head and body become covered with pollen. As it moves among flowers, the pollen stuck to the bat's fur is transferred to flowers on other plants, effecting cross-pollination. Cross-pollination is essential to the plant's reproduction. Plants that depend primarily on bats open at dusk and produce nectar attractive to bats. Flower shapes are often just right to receive a nectar bat's head. Even tall desert plants, like saguaro, organ pipe cacti, and agaves are highly dependent on bat pollinators.

Bats That Eat Fruit (frugivory)

Fruit bats are also extremely valuable to the maintenance and regeneration of tropical rain forests. These bats are attracted by the odors of ripe fruit, such as a fig. Picking a fruit with its mouth, a bat will fly off to eat its dinner. By discarding undigested seeds, bats help to distribute them to different parts of the forest. Some fruit bats eat up to two and a half times their body weight in food in a single night. Just one bat can deposit up to 60,000 seeds in a night. A small percentage of these will take root and grow into new trees. Fruit bats are also vital to forest regeneration in clear-cut areas, because they do not hesitate to cross clearings, dropping seeds as they fly. A high percentage of the woody plants that grow in cleared areas come from seeds dropped by bats.

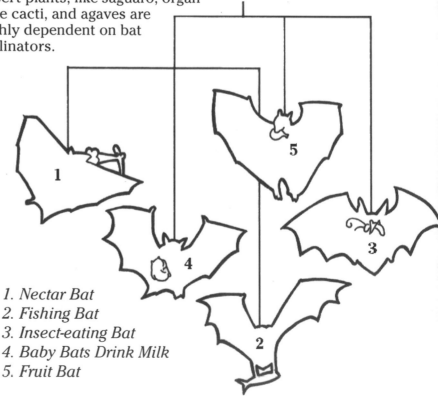

1. *Nectar Bat*
2. *Fishing Bat*
3. *Insect-eating Bat*
4. *Baby Bats Drink Milk*
5. *Fruit Bat*

Bats That Eat Insects (insectivory)

About 70% of bats are insectivorous. They are major predators of night-flying insects, including mosquitoes and crop pests such as corn borer and cutworm moths. Nursing mothers eat as much as their body weight in insects nightly. Bats chase insects using their echolocation (sonar). Insects may be caught directly in the mouth, can be deflected towards the mouth with the wings, or can be captured in the tail membrane. Where bats still exist in large numbers, they provide valuable insect control, chemical free and at no charge.

Bats That Eat Fish (piscivory)

Few people have heard of fishing bats. Most live in the Latin American tropics, where they fish over quiet streams and lagoons. Flying close to the water's surface, the bat uses its sonar to detect ripples and tiny exposed fins of minnows. Lowering its huge feet and gaff-like claws into the water, it grabs little fish out of the water. A single bat may eat 30 to 40 small fish in a night.

Baby Bats Feed on Milk

Being mammals, baby bats nurse from nipples located on their mother's chest. Babies nurse for several weeks before they learn to fly and find food on their own. Mother's milk is extremely high in fat content. It is thought that only marine mammals have more fat. When necessary, babies can hitch a ride on mom as she flies. Baby bats have large feet that they use to cling onto the mother's fur, and milk teeth that attach to the nipple so they can hang on tight. As babies grow they become too heavy for moms to carry. Mothers return to nurse them several times a night. Most bats produce only one baby per year.

Fruit Bat

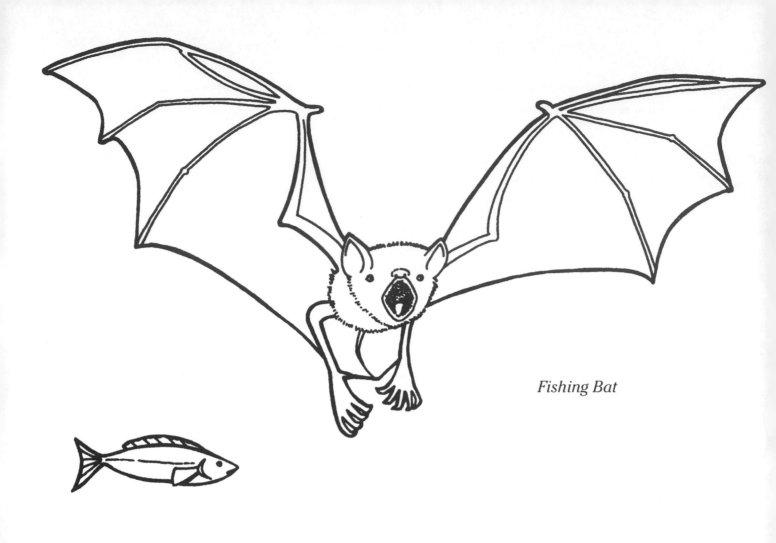

Fishing Bat

Nectar Bat

Baby Bats Drink Milk

Insect-eating Bat

HOW A BAT COMPARES TO ME

Objective: *To compare anatomy and physiology of bats and humans*

Grades: *3-5*

Type of Activity: *Taking measurements*

Materials:
- *Copies of page 43*
- *Pencils*
- *Clock with seconds*
- *Weight scale for humans*
- *Gram scale*
- *Tape measures*

Background Information

Children can learn a great deal about bats and themselves by comparing various aspects of their anatomy, physiology, and behavior. In this activity, children take their own measurements and compare them to those of bats.

Mammals

Even though bats fly and people walk on the ground, bats and people are similar in many ways. That's because both people and bats are mammals. With few exceptions, all mammals give birth to live young, nurse babies with milk, and have hair. Other mammals include dogs, cats, chipmunks, raccoons, elephants, monkeys, and whales.

Wingspan

Bat wingspans vary from about seven inches to nearly six feet. Most bats are small mammals, although the flying fox bats achieve a large size. The world's largest bat is a flying fox from Southeast Asia. The mask on page 28 illustrates why this bat is called a flying fox. Its face is very similar to a fox or dog. It feeds entirely on fruit. Have children outstretch their arms and measure the distance between finger tips.

Number of Fingers

A bat's wing is actually a modified hand. Refer to the diagram on page 37 and explain how the wing bones are actually greatly elongated fingers. Also point out the thumb. The thumb has a small claw which aids the bat in crawling around on rough surfaces.

Weight

Have children get on a scale and take their own weight. The world's smallest bat (the bumblebee bat from Thailand) weighs only two grams, less than a penny. The majority of bats weigh less than 50 grams, about two ounces.

Resting Heart Rate

Using a clock with a seconds indicator, demonstrate to students how to find their pulse (by putting your fingers against the carotid artery in the neck). Sitting down, students should take a resting pulse by counting the number of heart beats in a 15 second period and multiplying this by four to determine the total for one minute.

Active Heart Rate

Before taking this rate, have children simulate flight by doing one minute of jumping jacks. Immediately following this, they take their pulse again using the method described above. The bat's heart rate is high because flight is hard work. Its heart must pump rapidly to provide lots of oxygen, which is carried to flight muscles by blood. During hibernation, the opposite extreme, a bat's heart rate slows to only 20 heart beats per minute.

Wing Beats

To determine wing beats per second, have the children flap their arms like wings and count the number they can do in five seconds. The teacher then divides that number by five to find the rate per second. To support a body in the air and overcome the force of gravity, a flying animal must beat its wings very quickly (perhaps 12 times a second) to maintain altitude. How does the children's rate compare to the bat's? Some very large bats are capable of soaring on the wind, just like hawks and eagles.

Food Consumption

The teacher will need to help students determine this number ($\frac{1}{32}$ of child's weight). Flying fox bats eat about two and a half times their own body weight in fruit in a night. Have the children weigh themselves, and with the help of the teacher, calculate how many pounds of food they would have to eat if they ate like a fruit bat. Insectivorous bats eat about half their weight in insects each night.

Lifespan

The average lifespan for a human is 74 years. Banding records have shown than some insectivorous bats live up to 32 years or more. For their size, bats are among the longest lived animals. For comparison, most mice have a lifespan of only about two years.

HOW A BAT COMPARES TO ME

	Student	Bats
Kind of Animal	_____	mammal
Wingspan (armspan)	_____	6 ½ inches, bumblebee bat from Thailand; almost six feet for the great flying fox from Java
Number of Fingers	_____	four fingers, and one thumb
Weight	_____	most bats weigh less than two ounces or 56 grams
Heart Beats/Minute Resting	_____	less than 100
Heart Beats/Minute Active	_____	as many as 900
Wing Beats/Second	_____	12 for a little brown bat
Food Consumption	_____ one to five pounds, about ¹/₃₂ of body weight	flying fox bats can eat 2 ½ times their body weight in one night
Lifespan	_____	some bats live 30 years or more

12 BAT FRUIT SALAD

Objective: *To understand how bats are important to products we use every day*

Grades: *K-5*

Type of Activity: *Food preparation*

Materials:
- *Mixing bowl*
- *Spoons for mixing, serving, and eating*
- *Knives*
- *Napkins*
- *Selection of food items from the list*

Background Information

Few people realize how many products they use every day depend in some way on bats. These include hardwoods, balsa wood, spices, dyes, fibers, and many food items. Some plants depend directly on bats for pollination or seed dispersal. Others, like banana plants and peach trees, no longer need bats in a direct sense since the commercial varieties do not require pollination (bananas) or seed dispersal (bananas and peaches). But the genetic ancestors of these varieties still depend directly on bats. Should there be a need to improve disease resistance, agriculturists must obtain new genes from ancestral types. So bats are still very important to the crop. (See Activity 1 for a discussion of bats and economics.)

This activity is designed to focus on the many benefits bats provide to people. The fruit salad is made up of food items that are in some way bat- dependent. Wild bananas are both pollinated and dispersed by flying foxes, while figs, carob, peaches, dates, and mangos rely on them only for seed dispersal. The seeds of guavas and cashews are dispersed by leaf-nosed bats.

Quantities of the items used will depend on the size of the group so no amounts are listed. During food preparation, encourage the children to talk about the many benefits bats provide both to the environment and to humanity.

Products from Bat-dependent Plants

bananas	peaches
mangos	figs
dates	cashews
carob	canned guavas

Steps

1. Purchase a selection of food items from the list.

2. Cut the fruit into bite-sized pieces and place in a large mixing bowl.

3. Mix in peach or banana yogurt.

4. Sprinkle with chopped cashews and carob chips

5. Serve in paper cups

13 WHERE'S MY BABY?

Objective: *To learn how mother free-tailed bats find their babies*

Grades: *2-4*

Type of Activity: *Game*

Materials:
- *Cotton balls*
- *Variety of scents from the list*
- *Blindfolds*

Background Information

In the southwestern U.S., Mexican free-tailed bats roost together in large numbers. A cave in Central Texas is home to 20 million free-tails. Most of these are females and in early June each produces a single young, approximately doubling the size of the colony. Hundreds of square feet of cave wall space are carpeted with bat pups. Born without fur, the babies pack tightly together in densities of up to 500 per square foot to share body heat and stay warm. Mothers usually roost together in another part of the cave, each returning to nurse her baby several times a day.

For many years scientists believed that mothers probably fed any youngster they found. Recently, a study demonstrated that each mother actually locates her own baby through recognition of its scent and call. This is amazing considering the fact that they must find their own amidst millions of other active mothers and babies.

This game enables children to play the roles of mothers and babies trying to find each other in a dark, noisy situation. The whole class participates, but only

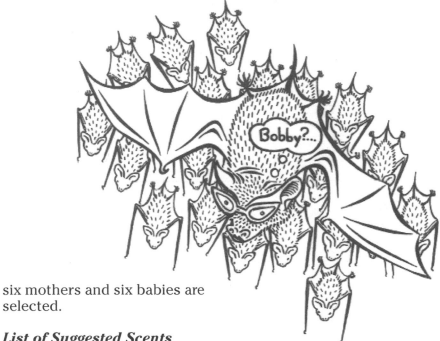

six mothers and six babies are selected.

List of Suggested Scents

Vinegar	Vanilla
Cinnamon	Perfume
Garlic	Banana

Rules

1. Select six mothers and six babies.

2. Each baby is given a cotton ball with a scent (see scent list for suggestions). The mother needs to become acquainted with the smell.

3. The baby is then assigned a call, some simple pattern of a tongue-clicking. Mother and baby should practice several times to ensure recognition of scent and sound.

4. Mothers are then blindfolded.

5. The other students in the class are also babies but without a scent or assigned call. All babies are arranged in an open space, and the teacher places the six special babies throughout the group. All babies are stationery and must not move. Only the mothers will move.

6. The blindfolded mothers are assisted to the edge of the group. Now they must find their own baby. All babies call, clicking at random without a pattern, except for the six babies who must use the pattern they practiced with the six mothers. Babies are hungry so they should click loudly.

7. If a mother bumps into a designated "baby," the baby is required to place the cotton ball near the nose of the mother, otherwise no contact is made.

8. The winner is the mother and baby who find each other first. When pairs find each other they should leave the circle. The game is over when all mothers and babies are reunited.

14 BAT MATH

Objective: *To use math skills to solve problems dealing with the ecology of bats*

Grades: *4-5*

Type of Activity: *Mathematics*

Materials:
- *Paper*
- *Pencil*

Background Information

Many interesting aspects of bat biology can be taught through solving math problems. The following exercises can also be used as models on which to create additional mathematical problems for any age group. Teachers can select problems appropriate for the class's ability.

1. A little brown bat can flap its wings 12 times a second. How many times can it flap in one minute? In 15 minutes? (720, 10,800)

2. A human's active heart beat is 150 times a minute. For a bat it is 900 per minute. How much faster does the bat's heart beat? How many times does a bat's heart beat a second? (750, 15)

3. A little brown bat can catch 600 mosquitoes in one hour. How many can it catch in 2 ½ hours? (1,500)

4. Twenty little brown bats live in a bat house. If one can catch 600 mosquitoes in an hour, and providing there was an abundant supply of mosquitoes, how many could all the bats catch in 3 hours? (36,000)

5. A bat's heart rate when active is 900 beats a minute. When it hibernates the rate drops to about 20 per minute. How much does it slow down? How many times will a hibernating bat's heart beat in one day (24 hours)? (880, 28,800)

6. Insectivorous bats can eat half their weight in insects each night, including many agricultural and yard pests — moths for example. If the bat weighs 16 grams and a moth weighs 0.4 grams, how many moths will the bat eat before it is full? If the bat ate only moths, how many moths could it eat from May to September, about 150 days? (20, 3,000)

7. A flying fox bat can eat 2 ½ times its weight in fruit in a night. If you were to do the same, how many pounds of food would you eat in a night? (student's weight times 2.5)

8. A Sonoran Desert bat pollinates the flowers on 12 different Saguaro cacti in one night. How many cacti will it pollinate in 30 nights? (360)

9. Fruit bats live in the tropics and discard the seeds after eating a meal. A rain forest bat can disperse 60,000 seeds in just one night. If it has dispersed 480,000 seeds, how many nights must it have been feeding? (8)

10. Mexican free-tailed bats in Texas produce just one baby each year. How many babies will a colony of five million females produce in one summer? If half the babies are eaten by predators and/or die during the long fall migration back to Mexico, how many are left? If one quarter of the remaining young die in their winter roost or during the spring migration back to Texas, how many young will return? (5 million, 2.5 million, 1,875,000)

11. A colony of 10,000 endangered gray bats can eat 30 million insects in a night. These bats hibernate in caves in the southern U.S. If, during the winter, repeated disturbance by people caused the bats to burn body fat needed to keep them alive until spring, and 3,000 bats starved to death, how many would be left and how many insects would they eat in a night? How many insects would remain uneaten? (7,000, 21 million, 7 million)

12 × 12 = 144

15 A YEAR IN THE LIFE OF LITTLE BROWN BATS

Objective: *To become familiar with the lifestyle of one bat species over the course of a year*

Grades: *4-5*

Type of Activity: *Lecture and discussion*

Materials:
- *Calendar*
- *Paper*
- *Pencils*
- *Notebook (optional)*

Background Information

This activity can be utilized as a study unit or can be spread out over the course of a year. The teacher presents the material to students in four distinct segments and leads a discussion using suggested topics. The educator can plan a presentation around each season, bringing the students up-to-date about activities in the lives of little browns at that particular time of year. Students may wish to keep a notebook and record what is happening to the bats during different seasons. Additional information, such as seasonal weather conditions and what other animals are doing this time of year can also be included.

A Year in the Life of Little Brown Bats, *Myotis lucifugus*

Introduction

The little brown bat is one of the most abundant species in the U.S. and Canada, found coast to coast in the northern two-thirds of the U.S. A small bat, weighing less than half an ounce, it is one kind of bat frequently found roosting in human dwellings. While not everyone wants bats in their attic, little browns do make good neighbors. When mosquitoes are abundant, a single bat can catch up to 600 in just one hour.

The study of bats reveals creatures far more amazing in fact than their portrayal by myth and legend might suggest. The little brown is one of almost 1,000 species that make up the second largest order of mammals, Chiroptera, (see Activity 8). Bat species represent about one quarter of the world's mammals.

Like most mammals, including people, little brown bats have hair, give birth to live young, and feed their babies with milk. Baby bats nurse from two nipples located on the mother's breasts.

Bats are unique among mammals because they are the only ones that can fly. Their forearm and hand evolved into a "hand wing," which is the meaning of the order's name. The wing is formed by membranous skin stretched between elongated finger bones. The clawed thumb is separate from the wing and is used for clinging. Little browns, along with many other bat species, also have a membrane between their hind legs called an interfemoral membrane. It helps a bat to maneuver in flight and to scoop up insects. A bat's legs are adapted for hanging, and they use little muscular effort to hang upside down. Their toes have sharp, curved-under claws that hook onto rough surfaces.

Sonar, or echolocation, (see Activity 4) enables little browns and other bats to use dark caves for roosts, to fly at night without collisions, and to locate prey. Night flight allows bats to avoid daytime predators and to take advantage of a variety of food sources without competition from diurnal feeding birds.

Little brown bats, along with snakes, spiders, and other misunderstood and feared animals, have suffered from centuries of myth and superstition. Their ability to fly and maneuver in complete darkness has often been portrayed as unnatural or evil. Bats also have been associated with the spookiness of Halloween, adding to the misconception that all bats are vampires and that they all suck the blood of their prey. In reality, little brown bats, like other bat species, are clean, gentle, and fascinating animals as well as being very important to the environment.

Part I. FALL

During the summer months, bats have been consuming great numbers of insects (about half their weight in insects each night) and putting on body fat that will be utilized during a long hibernation. By August, adults and juveniles depart summer roosts and begin migration to winter hibernation sites. The sexes have been apart for the summer, females rearing young in maternity colonies, males roosting nearby as solitary individuals or in bachelor colonies. Banding studies have shown that some little browns migrate more than 200 miles between summer and winter roosts. They can cover more than 20 miles in a single night. Distance traveled probably depends on availability of wintering sites. Their homing ability enables them to return to the same hibernation location year after year.

In late August, male and female little brown bats of all ages begin to "swarm" near hibernation caves. This congregation of bats in flight may represent some form of orientation behavior, helping to advertise to others suitable hibernation sites, especially inexperienced juveniles. Bats seek out the few caves that provide proper temperature and humidity conditions needed for hibernation. The cave's winter temperature is critical. A cave that is too warm would not enable a bat to enter a deep hibernation, and in very cold temperatures the bats could freeze to death.

Before hibernation, when little browns are in peak physical condition, they mate, setting the stage for the next generation. The female retains live sperm in her reproductive tract while she hibernates; ovulation and fertilization are delayed until she becomes active in the spring. Growing a fetus would be extremely difficult without food to eat and while spending most of the winter in a deep hibernation (low metabolic) state.

STUDENT ACTIVITIES FOR Part I, FALL

Discussion:

1. **What is migration?** (A seasonal round-trip journey by an animal.)

2. **What is homing?** (Ability to return directly to the home location when displaced.)

3. **What are some advantages of migration?** (Changing location seasonally helps to find more abundant food and water resources, locate mates, and find appropriate roosting conditions.)

4. **What animals other than bats migrate?** (Birds, whales, turtles, fish, monarch butterflies.)

5. **What is a swarm? Give some examples.** (A group of animals gathering in large numbers, for example, many kinds of insects.)

Writing:

1. You are a bat flying 100 miles to your winter roost. What are the advantages of going there? What kinds of problems might you encounter getting there?

2. What are some possible differences between what bats and people do in the fall to get ready for winter?

Part II. WINTER

As weather grows colder and days become shorter, insects become harder to find, and little brown bats enter hibernation in September or October. They locate a place in a cave where the temperature remains between 40-50°F (5-10°C) and humidity is 78% or more. High humidity helps prevent evaporative water loss from their body surface (dehydration). They hook their claws into the cave ceiling or walls, hang upside down, and go into a deep hibernation sleep.

All bodily functions slow down. Their heart rate slows to as low as 20 beats per minute, respiration decreases, and body temperature drops to that of the cave wall. By roosting in constantly cool places and allowing body temperature to fall to that of the cave, little brown bats can dramatically lower their metabolism. This enables them to survive for from six to eight months on very little

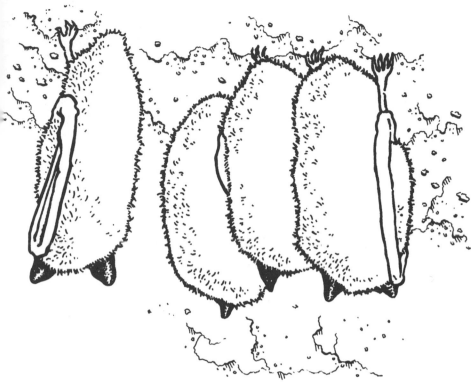

energy. While winter wears on, they live on the energy stored in body fat reserves.

Like other mammalian hibernators, bats do not remain asleep for the whole winter but wake up from time to time to urinate and drink. Moisture from cave walls and condensation droplets on their fur are the usual sources of water. Uninterrupted sleep for little browns averages between 12 and 19 days but may last as long as 83 days. Drafts and changes in temperature will arouse bats, and they may respond by moving to a new location. Increased energy demands created by too frequent arousal may deplete fat stored to the point where they die from starvation. For this reason, it is important never to disturb bats that are hibernating. Any human activity in their winter caves reduces their chance of surviving until spring. Cues to end hibernation probably include depletion of fat reserves and rising cave temperatures.

STUDENT ACTIVITIES FOR Part II, WINTER

Discussion:

1. **What is hibernation?** (The dormant or torpid state in which there is a dramatically slowed body metabolism, such as a reduced heart and respiration rate.)

2. **What are the advantages of hibernation?** (Preserving energy resources to stay alive until food supply and weather are favorable.)

3. **Name some animals that hibernate.** (Some bats, woodchucks, frogs, some insects, etc.)

4. **How do human beings respond to winter?** (Add clothing, move about and exercise to keep warm, consume more calories, stay inside warm shelter, migrate to warmer states like Florida.)

Writing:

1. What are some things that you do in wintertime? Are they at all similar to what bats do?

2. How long can you stay asleep at one time? What would wake you up? Is it different for a bat?

Part III. SPRING

As spring approaches, little brown bats gradually arouse from their deep sleep and make short flights within the cave. As females emerge and begin to feed, ovulation takes place and fertilization is accomplished by sperm that have been stored since mating took place in the fall. Females are now pregnant and usually give birth within two months after fertilization. The gestation period is not fixed, as in most mammals, but varies depending on favorable climate and availability of sufficient quantities of food.

In early April, the pregnant females begin their spring migration to summer roosting sites, often in attics, barns, or other buildings where they establish maternity colonies with often between 300-600 other females. Banding studies show that they return to the same sites each year. The males either roost alone or form small separate colonies by themselves. Little brown bats can survive in attics that are as hot as 103°F (42°C). In extreme heat situations, bats utilize several techniques to cool off, including moving to cooler places within the attic during the heat of the day. Warm sites with relatively stable temperatures are preferred for raising young, which is why buildings are frequently used.

When it is time to give birth in June and July, the females hang on to the roost with their thumbs and feet and help catch their newborns in their interfemoral (tail) membranes. The baby, whose eyes do not open for two days, immediately uses its large thumbs and hind feet to climb up and firmly attach its mouth to a nipple.

Little brown bats produce only one baby per year. This is true for most species, making bats the slowest reproducing mammals for their size. But, relative to other mammals, bats are enormous at birth. Baby little browns may weigh as much as 30% of the mother's weight. A similar ratio of newborn to mother's weight in humans would mean a 120-pound woman would bear a 36-pound infant!

At dusk, mothers leave young behind in the roost and return between foraging flights to nurse their own offspring, apparently recognizing the infant's particular smell and individual chirping call. The baby bats grow rapidly, gaining approximately 18% of their birth weight each day. During lactation, mothers eat increasing amounts of food, up to their body weight in insects each night. Young little browns are able to fly in about three weeks but continue to nurse for a week or more after they begin learning to forage on their own. This delay in weaning probably provides important nutritional support for the juveniles while they improve their hunting skills.

Females usually reach sexual maturity by the end of the first summer and males mature in about 16 months. Banding has shown that it is not unusual for both sexes to live 10 years or more. Some have lived for more than 32 years, making them the longest lived mammals on earth for their size.

STUDENT ACTIVITIES FOR Part III, SPRING

Discussion:

1. **What are some comparisons between human and bat pregnancies?** (Gestation length is nine months in human beings and about two months in little brown bats; both are mammals, and in both the fetus is nourished by a placenta while growing in the uterus.)

2. Sometimes fetal growth rate is slowed down in bats due to poor weather and availability of food. **Is it possible for pregnant women to affect the development of the fetus?** (Somewhat; positive effects may be gained by receiving good prenatal care, not smoking or drinking alcohol or using harmful drugs, but they can't appreciably alter the length of pregnancy.)

3. **How do you differ from bats in keeping cool when the temperature is hot?** (You perspire, put on lighter clothing, use electric fans or air conditioning, drink liquids; little brown bats do not sweat or pant, but they can move vertically to lower and cooler places within the roost.)

Writing:

1. Imagine that you are a bat living in an attic. What do you think might be some of your adventures? What would you do if you saw a human coming?

2. What kinds of things must a young bat learn on its very first flight?

Part IV. SUMMER

Summer is a crucial period in the life of little brown bats. Finding enough food to eat will, in large part, determine their survival for the next year. Without a significant amount of additional body fat from feeding on the summer's supply of insects, the bats will not have the reserves they need to survive the winter. This is especially true for youngsters.

Little brown bats forage about two hours after sunset and two more hours just before sunrise. They usually make several passes each night through a particular "beat" near ponds and streams. They listen to the cries of other bats to help locate new sources of food, preferring moths, beetles, mosquitoes, and flies. The average insect eaten weighs about two milligrams. Insects are caught, on average, at the rate of about one every eight seconds. Between hunts, the bats rest in night roosts, often crevices, where they form tight clusters. During heavy rainstorms or high winds, bats save energy by making shorter hunting flights, delaying take-off, or not flying at all. They also save energy by going into torpor, a physiological state similar to hibernation when metabolic body functions slow down.

Finding enough to eat isn't always easy. Because bats fly at night, they must use echolocation to navigate in the dark and find food. (See Activity 4 for a more complete discussion of echolocation.) Echolocation, also called sonar, utilizes a system of sending out sound pulses through the mouth which, as they bounce off objects, are reflected back to the bat's ears as echoes. Little browns can process information about their immediate vicinity instantaneously, enabling them to zig zag through the trees and chase an insect at the same time.

Some insects have developed methods for avoiding bats. Certain insects, like noctuid moths, have a type of ear that can detect a bat's echolocation calls. Upon hearing a nearby bat, they often take an evasive action like making a nose dive towards the ground.

In addition to chasing darting insects through the night, bats must also avoid predators, like hawks and owls, and pay attention to changing weather.

STUDENT ACTIVITIES FOR Part IV, SUMMER
Discussion:

1. **What is echolocation or sonar?** (SONAR is an acronym from "sound navigation ranging," a system developed by scientists to locate objects under water by sending out signals and listening to the echo. Although sonar was described by humans, bats and other animals have been using the system for a very long time.) **How long have bats used this technique?** (Fossils of relatively modern bats have been found that date back to the Eocene period, about 54 million years ago; the ability to echolocate probably developed gradually over millions of years.)

2. **Name some animals that use a form of sonar to find their way.** (Whales, dolphins, bats.)

3. **Do people use echolocation?** (The blind tap with a cane. Submarines use sonar to navigate the oceans.)

    4. Insects and other animals have learned to detect bat sonar and to reduce the odds of being caught.

What are some other ways by which prey evade predators? (By camouflage, possessing great speed for escape, distraction such as the squid's ink, and by performing some defensive behavior like the spraying of a skunk.)

Writing:

1. Pretend you are writing a newspaper article about why little brown bats are very beneficial. Include some interesting facts about their lives.

2. Conduct an interview with your family or neighbors to determine what people know about one of the most common bats in the U.S. Make a list of things you can do to help educate people about bats.

FOLLOW-UP ACTIVITIES

1. Visit a nearby nature center, zoo, or museum to find information on bats.

2. Look for bats flying over your yard at twilight. Keep a daily record of what you see, including observations on temperature, wind force and direction, and time of day. When did you see the last bat in the fall and first one in the spring?

3. Have a Bat Party (not just for Halloween), make bat cookies and party decorations with a bat motif.

4. In the library, use the *Reader's Guide to Periodical Literature* and the *Magazine Index* to look up articles about bats; check out books on bats. Use an atlas or globe to find places that are mentioned in connection with bats. For example, Carlsbad Caverns in New Mexico is home to several hundred thousand bats.

16 REFRIGERATOR BATS

Grades: *2-5*

Type of Activity: *Craft project*

Materials:
- *Stove or hot plate*
- *Mixing bowl*
- *Large spoon*
- *Plastic bag*
- *Wax paper*
- *Dinner knives*
- *Cornstarch*
- *Baking soda*
- *Water*
- *Acrylic sealer or clear nail polish*
- *Acrylic paints or markers*
- *Glue*
- *Small magnets (available at craft shop)*
- *Copies of bat shapes below, printed on card stock*

Background Information

Bats come in a variety of sizes, shapes, and colors. Children can cut around a copy of the diagrams below as models, or create a bat of their own imagination. The following names might also spark creativity:

> Spear-nosed bat
> Tube-nosed bat
> Yellow-winged bat
> Red bat
> Spotted bat
> Flying fox bat

Recipe for Approximately 10 4" Bats

(Prepare dough ahead of time)
2 cups cornstarch
4 cups baking soda
2 ½ cups cold water

Mix ingredients in a medium-sized saucepan and cook over medium heat, stirring constantly. Cook about 10 minutes or until the mixture is the consistency of mashed potatoes. Remove from heat, turn out onto a plate, and then cover with a damp cloth. After the dough cools, knead it gently into a smooth ball. Then store it in a tightly sealed plastic bag and refrigerate until you're ready to use it.

Steps to Making Bat Magnets

1. Using the palm of your hand, flatten a golf ball-sized lump of dough onto a piece of wax paper. The pressed dough should be at least ¼" thick. Don't press it too thin or the dough may break as it dries.

2. Mold the dough into the shape of a bat, using the diagrams included below for reference.

3. Make eyes, nose, ears or other features by adding tiny bits of dough or by carving them into the dough with a pencil point. Be careful not to push the pencil point too deeply or the dough may break after it dries.

4. Let dry overnight.

5. Carefully remove the bat shape from the wax paper and paint it with acrylic paints or color it with markers. Let dry. Once the bat is dry, paint with clear nail polish or acrylic sealer. This will help protect it and make it shine.

6. Glue one or two small magnets to the back of the bat.

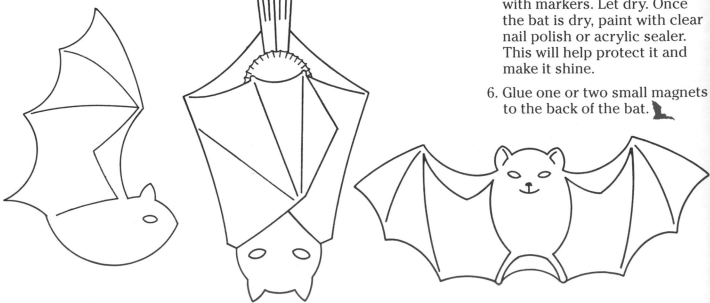

17 BAT RAP

Objective: *To convey important information about bats by creating and performing rap music routines*

Grades: *1-5*

Type of Activity: *Music*

Materials
- *Copies of page 54*
- *Paper*
- *Pencils*
- *Tape recorder (optional)*
- *Video camera (optional)*

Background Information

Rap music is very popular with young people and has been used to convey important information, for example that drugs are dangerous. The beat is catchy and kids often enjoy performing a rap in small groups.

On page 54 is an example of a "Fruit Bat Bad Rap" that can be copied and distributed to the class. Children can create their own rap about the many benefits of bats (insect predation, pollination, seed dispersal), or dispel many of the common myths (see Activities 1 and 2). Younger students can work with the teacher in creating a rap while older ones can work in small groups. This is a great activity for school Halloween programs.

18 BATS IN THE COMICS

Objective: *To create comic strips to communicate important information about bats*

Grades: *3-5*

Type of Activity: *Art and writing*

Materials:
- *Copies of pages 55 and 56*
- *Colored markers or pencils*

Background Information

Creating comic strips can be entertaining as well as a means to educate readers. This activity enables students to communicate what they have learned about bats. To maximize the impact, this exercise should be used following a thorough introduction to bats.

Copy the cartoon strip form on page 56. Using the two bat cartoon characters provided on this page (Billy and Brenda Bat), children can create an adventure story or have Billy and Brenda tell the readers about why bats are important. It will be helpful to have other comic strip examples available, for example comic books and Sunday funnies. Finished cartoon strips can then be posted for other students to enjoy.

Title

1

2

3

4

5

6

Asymptomatic carrier	An animal that can contract a disease and transmit it to other animals without showing symptoms itself.
Bachelor colony	A colony of bats composed mostly of males and nonbreeding females.
Carotid artery	Arteries located either side of the throat, which are the principal suppliers of blood to the head and neck. By placing fingers firmly over an artery, a pulse can be detected.
Chiroptera	The order of mammals that includes all bats. The word literally means "hand-wing." These are the only true flying mammals.
Diurnal	Active during the day.
Echolocation	The use of reflected sound from an emitter (such as a bat or dolphin) to locate objects.
Ecosystem	A major interacting system that involves both living organisms and their physical environment.
Flying foxes	Bats of the suborder Megachiroptera. They all have large eyes, eat primarily fruit or nectar, and generally lack echolocation ability. There are nearly 200 species, and they live only in tropical and subtropical climates of the Old World.
Frugivory	The habit of eating fruit.
Gestation	The period from conception to birth; that is, when the mother is pregnant.
Habitat	The locality in which a plant or animal lives.
Hibernation	A state of greatly reduced activity and metabolism produced by lowering of body temperature. It occurs in winter, enabling an animal to survive on stored fat reserves until spring.
Interfemoral membrane	The membrane that spans the area between a bat's legs, feet, and tail. Also called a tail membrane.
Insectivory	The habit of eating insects.
Maternity colony	A group of pregnant or nursing bats that gather into a single large colony, sometimes hundreds or even millions, for the purpose of rearing young. The shared body heat is essential to growth of the young.
Megachiroptera	One of the two suborders of Chiroptera, including a single family, the Pteropodidae. Known as flying foxes.

Microchiroptera One of the two suborders of Chiroptera. It includes nearly 800 species and 17 families of mostly small insect-eating bats. All bats living in the United States and Canada (and all of the Western Hemisphere) belong to this group. A few eat fruit, nectar, or other animals. This suborder also includes vampire bats.

Nectarivory The habit of eating nectar.

Nocturnal Active at night.

Nose leaf The fleshy flap of skin around the nostrils of some bats. It is usually triangular in shape and rises vertically from the tip of the nose.

Organ pipe A large desert cactus shaped like organ pipes and pollinated primarily by bats, and also by birds and bees.

Pollination The transfer of pollen from the anther of a flowering plant to the stigma prior to fertilization.

Rabies An infectious viral disease of mammals usually transmitted through a bite.

Saguaro Large columnar species of cactus found in the Sonoran Desert and pollinated by bats, birds, and bees.

Seed dispersal The act of transporting seeds from the parent plant to new locations where seeds are more likely to survive. When forests are cleared they cannot regenerate without seed dispersal.

Sonar SONAR is an acronym for "sound navigation ranging," a system developed by scientists to locate objects under water by sending out signals and listening to the echo. Also known as echolocation.

Tail membrane The membrane that spans the area between a bat's legs, feet, and tail, often referred to as the interfemoral membrane.

Thermals A rising body of warm air resulting from the sun heating up the earth.

Torpor A state of reduced activity and metabolism similar to hibernation but not necessarily associated with a particular season. Many bats, unlike most other mammals, can enter torpor to save energy at almost any time.

Ultrasonic Having a frequency above the human ear's audibility limit of about 20,000 cycles per second.

TOPICS FEATURED IN EACH ACTIVITY

Activity Name	*Topic*
1. Test Your Bat Q	General introduction to bats
2. Bat Attitude	Myths about bats
3. Bat Crossword Puzzles	Bat terminology
4. Seeing with Your Ears	Echolocation
5. Close Encounter with a Bat	Warning not to handle bats
6. Going, Going, Gone	Bat endangerment
7. Bat Masks	Bat diversity, facial anatomy
8. Greetings from a Bat	Scientific classification of bats
9. Bat Cave Bulletin Board	Bat anatomy, cave-dwelling bats
10. What's for Dinner?	Bat diets
11. How a Bat Compares to Me	Anatomy, physiology of bats, and kids
12. Bat Fruit Salad	Benefits of bats
13. Where's My Baby?	Mother and baby interactions
14. Bat Math	Bat ecology math problems
15. A Year in the Life...	Lifestyle of a common bat
16. Refrigerator Bats	
17. Bat Rap }	Summary activities, best used
18. Bats in the Comics	*after* an introduction to bats

READING LIST

Suggested Books for Younger Readers

Bash, Barbara. 1993. *Shadows of the Night: The Hidden World of the Little Brown Bat.* Sierra Club Books for Children, San Francisco, 30 pages.
With easy-to-read text and glowing water colors, the author paints a beautiful picture of a year in the life of a little brown bat, dispelling the mystery that surrounds these harmless creatures of the night. For grades 2-5.

*Cannon, Janell. 1993. *Stellaluna.* Harcourt Brace & Company, New York, 48 pages.
1994 Winner of the American Bookseller's Book of the Year (ABBY) Award; a beautifully illustrated story of friendship and discovery about a young fruit bat, separated from her mother and raised by birds. For all ages.

de Mauro, Lisa. 1990. *Explorer Books: Bats.* Bantam Doubleday Publishing Group, New York, 60 pages.
A factual account of bat diversity throughout the world. Easy-to-read text is complemented with black and white photos by Merlin Tuttle. For grades 4-10.

Halton, Cheryl M. 1991. *Those Amazing Bats.* Dillon Press Inc., Minneapolis, 96 pages.
Describes diversity, behavior, and benefits of bats. Features the work of Merlin Tuttle, bat house plans, appendix of endangered bats, and glossary. For grades 4-6.

Hopf, Alice L. 1985. *Bats.* Dodd, Mead & Co., New York, 64 pages.
An interesting introduction to the world of bats, including bats from around the globe, why they are valuable, their diversity, and behavior. Illustrated with black-and-white photos by Merlin Tuttle. For grades 5-8.

Horowitz, Ruth. 1991. *Bat Time.* Four Winds Press, New York, 32 pages.
A lyrical bedtime story relates the warmth and wonder of a family's shared appreciation for nighttime creatures, including bats. Richly illustrated with colored-pencil drawings. For grades K-4.

Jarrell, Randall. 1963. *The Bat Poet.* Macmillian Publishing Co., New York, 43 pages.
A funny and touching story of a little brown bat who discovers the world around him by writing poems about the animals living nearby. It is illustrated with delightful pen-and-ink drawings. For children of all ages.

Johnson, Sylvia A. 1985. *Bats.* Lerner Publications Co., Minneapolis, 48 pages.
Winner of the New York Academy of Sciences Children's Science Book Award; an appealing introduction to the habits of bats and the many ways bats benefit humans. Color photographs throughout. For grades 4-8.

*Lollar, Amanda. 1992. *The Bat in My Pocket.* Capra Press, California, 86 pages.
Animal lovers of all ages will be fascinated by the details of bat behavior in this true story of the rapport between the author and an injured Mexican free-tailed bat she rescues. Includes bat house plans. For all ages.

*Lovett, Sarah. 1991. *Extremely Weird Bats.* John Muir Publications, Santa Fe, 50 pages.
Easy-to-read text and colorful line drawings depict 21 of the world's most interesting and unusual bat species. Large color photos by Merlin Tuttle and colorful drawings. For grades 2-5.

*Milton, Joyce. 1993. *Bats: Creatures of the Night.* Grosset & Dunlap Inc., New York, 48 pages.
Accompanied by colorful and clever paper illustrations, the large, simple text covers a broad range of basic bat facts from anatomy to roosting and feeding habits. Designed to improve reading skills. For grades K-3.

Pringle, Laurence. 1991. *Batman: Exploring the World of Bats.* Charles Scribner's Sons, New York, 48 pages.
Traces Merlin Tuttle's fascination with bats from his youth to present. It tells how he became a nature photographer and founded Bat conservation International. This account of an exceptional scientist at work is illustrated with 24 of Tuttle's outstanding color photographs of bats. Substantial information about bat biology and conservation needs is included. For grades 5-12.

*Rink, Deane and Linda C. Wood. 1989. "Bats." Zoobooks. Wildlife Education Ltd., San Diego, 17 pages.
Full-color pages loaded with photographs and illustrations about bats. Includes myths about bats, anatomy, diet, ecological roles, and diversity, plus games and activities. For grades 1-4.

*Stuart, Dee. 1994. Bats: Mysterious Flyers of the Night. Carolrhoda Books, Inc., Minneapolis, 45 pages.
A thorough explanation of bats with striking color photographs by Merlin Tuttle on every page. Descriptions of feeding, migration, birth, and more introduce younger readers to 19 new vocabulary words. For grades 2-4.

Books for Educators and Older Students

Barbour, R.W. & W.H. Davis. 1969. Bats of America. University Press of Kentucky, Lexington, 286 pages.
Provides species descriptions for all bats found in the U.S. Includes information on range, habitat, behavior, food and feeding, and reproduction. Includes a bibliography and key to identification.

*Fenton, M.B. 1992. Bats. Facts on File, New York, 207 pages.
A well-illustrated introduction to the diversity of bats presented in a full-color format. Fully examines the status and study of bats around the world today. Contains information about echolocation, migration, foraging strategies, roosting behavior, social organization, population dynamics, public health, and conservation.

*Graham, G.L. 1994. Bats of the World, A Golden Guide Publication. Golden Press, New York, 151 pages.
A detailed, full-color introduction to 18 families of bats as well as many bat issues and facts.

Hill, J.B. and J.D. Smith. 1984. Bats: A Natural History. University of Texas Press, Austin, 243 pages.
This reference book covers many aspects of bat biology. Its global scope contains information about bats throughout the world, including maps showing distribution of bat families and line drawings of anatomy.

Kunz, T.H. (Ed.). 1982. Ecology of Bats. Plenum Press, New York and London, 425 pages.
Contributions from the world's foremost bat biologists make this volume essential reading for all serious students of bat biology. Contents include chapters on roosting ecology, reproduction, growth and survival, physiology, morphology, feeding behavior, bat/plant interactions, and more.

Kunz, T.H. (Ed.). 1988. Ecological and Behavioral Methods for the Study of Bats. Smithsonian Institution Press, Washington DC, 533 pages.
Topics covered include bat capture, care in captivity, marking and observational techniques, radiotelemetry, photography, age determination, reproductive assessment, and allozyme techniques for kinship assessment. The detailed chapters are clearly written, well illustrated, and include extensive bibliographies. Addresses for equipment and supplies are included.

Richarz, K. and A. Limbrunner. 1993. The World of Bats. Franck-Kosmos Verlags-GMBH & Co., Stuttgart, Germany (English translation by W. Charlton, THF Publications), 192 pages.
Well illustrated. Covers general information on bat behavior and ecology worldwide, with greater detail on European species. Includes a section on "Bats and Humankind" that explains the roles of bats in local economies and folklore.

*Tuttle, M.D. 1988. America's Neighborhood Bats. University of Texas Press, Austin, 96 pages.
An excellent introduction to American bats, covering a wide range of issues from public health and nuisance concerns to bat values and conservation needs. Common North American bats are featured with natural history information, color photographs, and a key to identification.

*Available from Bat Conservation International, P.O. Box 162603, Austin, TX 78716
1-800-538-BATS

EDUCATIONAL MATERIALS

From Bat Conservation International

Audiovisual Programs

From the tiny bumblebee bat to giant flying foxes, bats of all descriptions are shown hunting prey, pollinating flowers, and rearing their young in these spectacular slide shows and still-image videos. All programs emphasize the roles bats play in the balance of nature, featuring Merlin Tuttle's stunning close-up action photos. Unless otherwise noted, each program contains 80 images with a running time of about 15 minutes. Slide/tape programs include tape-cassette narration with auto-sync advance and sound-beeped manual advance. Or you can get the audio and images together on convenient VHS cassette. Scripts are available for review.

"Bats: Myth and Reality" – an introduction to bats of the world
       AV-1. slide/tape $85   AV-2. VHS video $19.95

"Bats of America" – a comprehensive look at North American bats
       AV-3. slide/tape $85   AV-4. VHS video $19.95

"Los Murcielagos de America Latina" – a detailed look at Latin American bats including vampire control. (Spanish Language only)
       AV-5. slide/tape $85   AV-7. VHS video $27.95

"Very Elementary Bats" – exciting bat facts especially for very young children (42 images, 7 minutes, video only)
       AV-8. VHS video $17.95

Mini-slide Sets

Perfect additions to complement an existing program or to stand alone as a short unit on bats. Ten images with supplementary text, no cassette narration.
AV-12. "Threatened and Endangered Bats of North America" slides $15.95
AV-13. "Common Bats of North America" slides $15.95

The Secret World of Bats

Originally shown on CBS television, this 48-minute live-action film is a must for naturalists, educators, and anyone interested in learning the fascinating truth about bats. World-renowned cinematographer Dieter Plage follows Bat Conservation International founder Merlin Tuttle across five continents, capturing all aspects of bat behavior with stunning slow motion photography, and introducing viewers to bat conservation issues.
AV-9. VHS video $41.95

Bats of America Poster

Features a collage of 21 of Merlin Tuttle's color photographs of 19 species found in North America. The poster illustrates bat diversity, important environmental roles bats play, and includes a conservation text. Its large size, 25"x36", and durable construction make this poster ideal for school and nature center use. P-4. $9.95

Bats: A Creativity Book for Young Conservationists by Jane F.G. Jennings.

With the focus on imagination, 28 activities challenge children in communication and math skills, writing, art, and more while increasing their understanding of bats. For ages 5-10. 30 pp. B-7. $3.95

America's Neighborhood Bats by Merlin Tuttle.

A perfect introduction to the wonderful world of bats by the founder of Bat Conservation International. Includes chapters on public health and nuisance concerns, basic biology, environmental values, conservation, and bat house construction. Common U.S. bats are featured with natural history information, beautiful color photographs, and a key to identification. 96pp. B-15. softcover, $10.95 B-14. hardcover, $20.95

The Bat House Builder's Handbook by Merlin Tuttle and Donna Hensley.
This handbook is the definitive source for bat house information. Based on research conducted by Bat Conservation International, it contains the results from the first-of-its-kind study on bat house occupancy. Includes three different sets of plans, research findings, tips for experimentation, answers to frequently asked questions, and information about the bats most likely to use bat houses. 36pp. BHG. $6.95

Ultrasound Bat Detector
A valuable tool for interpretive programs and backyard bat-watching; a must for serious educators. Sophisticated electronics translate high-frequency echolocation calls of bats to audible clicks, chirps, and beeps, allowing users to listen in on the bats in their areas. Imported from Europe. (Dollar fluctuation may necessitate price change without notice.) E-1. $265.00

Special Educator's Packages
Collections of educational materials at special prices. Save money and purchase a complete package with everything you'll need for a program on bats.

> SEP-3. Elementary Educator's Package $25.00
> Includes "Very Elementary Bats" video and "Educator's Activity Book about Bats."

> SEP-2. Standard Educator's Package $99.00
> Includes "Bats of America" color poster, "Bats of America" slide/tape program, "Educator's Activity Book about Bats," and a softcover edition of *America's Neighborhood Bats.*

Bat Fact Packs
With two sides of little-known facts, these wallet-sized fold-out cards are ideal to distribute for class projects, at lectures, or to interested friends. BP-1. Package of 25: $1.85 (includes postage and handling)
Quantities in multiples of 100: $6.40 ea. (includes postage and handling)

BCI Membership
Membership in Bat Conservation International is your introduction to a little-known world of nearly 1,000 of the earth's most intriguing animal species. You will receive a quarterly magazine that provides continuing education about bats, catalogues of new educational and gift products, invitations to join exclusive international ecotours in tropical locations, and opportunities to participate in workshops and field projects with Merlin Tuttle and other bat biologists.

> Friends of BCI Membership $40.00 (includes an exclusive thank-you gift)
> Basic Membership $30.00
> Educator/Student Membership $25.00

Except where listed, the above prices do not include postage and handling.

To order these items and/or to receive a free catalogue, contact
Bat Conservation International, P.O. Box 162603, Austin, TX 78716
1-800-538-BATS.

Published by Bat Conservation International, P.O. Box 162603, Austin, TX 78716 (512) 327-9721

Bat Conservation International is supported by tax-deductible contributions used for
public education, research, and conservation of threatened and endangered bats.

printed on recycled paper

Distributed by:

 UNIVERSITY OF TEXAS PRESS
PO Box 7819
Austin, TX 78713-7819

ISBN 0-292-70833-5

90000

9 780292 708334